"... AND GULLIVER RETURNS"

--In Search of Utopia--

Book 3

An Asian Utopia

KINO

BOOK 3

AN ASIAN UTOPIA

KINO

China's Beacon to the Future

by

Lemuel Gulliver XVI as told to Jacqueline Slow

© 2008

Dear friends—Obviously I wrote this series to be read from Book 1 to the end, but silly me! Readers often begin with what sounds interesting to them. This may leave them unaware of the characters, my friends and I. So let me introduce us. We were boyhood friends, as wild and as close as geese heading south for the winter. But our university educations split us philosophically like a drop of quicksilver hitting the floor. But like those balls of mercury, when brought together, they again become one. As have we.

Ray became a Catholic priest and moved far to the right of where our teenage liberalism had bound us. Ray calls himself a neo-conservative. We think he is a reactionary.

Lee slid to the left of our adolescent leanings, and somewhere along the line became an atheist. Lee is a lawyer.

Concannon, Con for short, retired from his very successful business. I guess his business experience moved him a bit to the right, to conservatism—a conservative just to the right of the middle.

Then there's me. I think I'm pretty much a middle of the roader—except for my passion to save our planet by reducing our population before global warming, massive poverty and far-reaching famines decimate our humanity. Hope this introduction makes our discussions make a bit more sense.

By the way, as most of you know, we have put our photos before every bit of dialogue. This should make you more familiar with us. So the books read more like plays. Since most of you read the books in PDF or EPUB format it is no problem. But if you read them in RTF or TXT you will probably lose the photos. This will make the transitions of the conversations more difficult to follow.   LG

TABLE OF CONTENTS

It took less than ten hours from Los Angeles International Airport to touch down in Jingjing, the capitol of Kino. From what I had remembered as a boy, Kino was a province of China but in the late 90s it had been granted a freedom to experiment with social and political policies and with technology. Its progress has been even more spectacular than that of China, which is so big that changing fast is very difficult. When Kino fails in an experiment it doesn't affect a billion people, as it did in China under the early communist dictators. Kino can move forward more quickly and find solutions to problems that work in a modern and globalized world.

Kino, as a new country, didn't have to endure the problems that plagued China during the 1900s. There were 40 years of war then 40 years of backward moving communism. But China is now making the progress that is rapidly bringing it to the leadership position of the world. Marco Polo would be proud. It practically owns the United States. The U.S. has bought trillions of dollars worth of Chinese goods and sold only a quarter of that amount to China. So China has been lending so much to the U.S. to keep it afloat that it practically owns New York and California!

China, of course, was a vast agricultural land with a rich cultural heritage, but a population crisis out of control. It had more than a billion people when I left Earth but it halved its yearly population increase. Here in Kino the 'one child' policy has been continued and modified. Kino now requires licenses to become parents.

In China the fertility rate has dropped to 1.7 per woman—less that the 2.1 that was once required required to replenish the parents and keep its population stable. By comparison the U.S. and U.K. fertility rates are 1.9 while Japan's is 1.4 and Hong Kong, Singapore and Hungary are at 1.3. Kino's fertility rate is only 1.2. On the other hand, most African countries, are in the 4 to 7 range, It is no wonder that so many want to escape north to Europe.

The millions of Chinese peasants of a few decades ago have been reduced as they have been absorbed by death or the cities. The uneducated masses have evolved into a highly educated citizenry which is astute in the ways of business and statesmanship. All this in a brief moment of history. It's like a cosmic Siegfried and Roy changing a paper tiger into a herd of lions at the snap of a finger. As effective as China has been, Kino is far ahead in its progress toward utopia.

Kino has had the opportunity to experiment in a modern "society based" society. That is, the rights of the society as a whole, rather than the rights of the individual citizens, are generally primary. They have also eliminated religion as a political force. A strong central government is in place. It requires the education of the citizens as to why improving the society will have more benefits for the average person than trying to pamper every individual's desires, which are so often called 'rights.' It makes me wonder if these individual 'rights', that are generally based on individual selfishness rather than the social good, are at least in part responsible for the over two million prison inmates in my country. The big question is where is the best balance between the desires of individuals and the overall good of one's society?

I was prepared to ride in a rickshaw from the airport, but my entourage and I were escorted from the jet by Madam Ching, the president of Kino, in a hydrogen powered limousine. There was no driver. The "electronic road grid" guided the car in and out of traffic. As we rode through the capital I was amazed by the cityscape. There were no rickshaws nor street sellers nor beggars. We sped along the elevated concrete freeways past tall steel and glass buildings which, I was told, were commercial enterprises and apartments. These buildings dwarfed those that I had seen many years ago in New York and Chicago. They were taller and broader than those with which I was familiar. But they were far more grand, not because of their immensity, but because of the touches of nature tastefully imbued into their architecture.

One edifice appeared to be that of a tree topped purple mountain, so familiar in the oriental paintings of days gone by. Another featured an immense waterfall cascading down its face. Larger than Niagara, more impressive than Yosemite, the silver falls bounced from level to level in a scene that even Nature couldn't match. And in the mists of the falls, at every level, the reflected rainbows of a thousand suns. The Sino-simplicity of the Tao in the opulence of modernity—the evolved excellence of the previous millennia of Oriental inspiration.

As we approached the capital building where I was to be greeted at a reception, I marveled at the cleanliness of the city. It was so different from the land I remembered in the America I left behind 20 years ago. And my brief glimpses of California last week did nothing to rinse the memories of the graffiti, the trash on the streets, and even the fear for one's life-- at home, in places of business, and even while driving. The selfish lack of concern by so many of my fellow citizens had soured me on the potentials of science and the hope of technology in delivering a utopian society to us. But here in Jingjing was a city, and perhaps even a whole country, that seemed to be able to rise above the commonplace and to produce caring responsible citizens who were able to enjoy the benefits of human knowledge and to perfect the potentials of humanhood.

I walked up the marble steps of the Great Hall, not knowing what to expect from my visit. As I passed through the gigantic bronze gateway, reminiscent of Ghiberti's towering doors of the Duomo's Baptistry, I mused, as did Michelangelo, that these "were fit to be the Gates of Paradise." While Ghiberti's masterpieces depicted the scenes from the Old Testament, these bronze doors of Kino depicted the age of civilization in both the East and the West. There were the depictions of Lao Tzu and Confucius from the East. There were the portrayals of the pharaohs' cultures. There was homage paid to the achievements of the university at Timbuktu and to the Muslim scholars to its east. There was a history of great philosophers of Greece—Democritus, Aristotle, Plato, Socrates. There were panels allotted to Genghis Khan, Alexander the Great, and yes, even to Mao. He was given a spot low on the gate. I wondered if it was because of his foundational work in developing the modern Chinese society or was he placed close to Hell because of the millions of Chinese he killed in his revolutionary quest.

The architects of splendor were recognized by their products--the Great Wall, the pyramids, the Parthenon, the Rhodes Colossus, the aqueducts of Rome. And there were Moses, Jesus, Mohammed, and of course, the Buddha. It was, indeed, like wandering through the vale of human history. And after having spent the last 20 years studying the annals of our recorded past, it was like a meeting with old friends.

Lucky for me, my language is still the major language of the elite of the world. My hosts were all able to converse with me. However their slang phrases escaped me. I guess that in my twenty years of travel a few new phrases had crept into the language. I had no idea of what was meant when one woman told me that my voyage had "frazzed" her. Or the young man who told me that my return had been a complete "gronsk" for his own education. With the world becoming smaller it was to be expected that slang from one language would invade that of another. But it left me completely "zerked." (Zerked, I found out is a Zuzu word for confused!)

It was not long before we were ushered into the dining area--a marbled hall reminiscent of old King Louie's Hall of Mirrors at Versailles. As the guest of honor I was seated by the President, the Minister of the People, and her husband. There must have been five hundred guests seated at these lace topped tables. The October afternoon sun sparkled from the crystal chandeliers and reflected in the wine goblets at my place. It strained my mind to realize that less than thirty years ago this land was a part of a communist country, where a few Communists ruled millions of peasants tending their rice paddies on the hillsides and in the valleys. In less than four decades these people had risen from a backward farming economy to perhaps the greatest economic power the world has known. How did this happen?

Madam Ching, as the Minister of the People, was the perfect person of whom to inquire about the control of population. Luckily she was eager to answer my queries. Of course she had a few of her own for me. She was interested in the questions of space--what did the planet Venus look like, how does it feel to be weightless, and what did I do to avoid boredom during those twenty years. Of course I was interested in how her country had come so far in the few short years since I had left. There was no question that the progress of Kino in the last thirty years was of far more import for the human race than was my voyage into space.

GLOBAL POLICIES

While the control of population was fascinating, I wanted to know a bit about the global policies of Kino and China during the last 30 years. I remember that even then, before their technological explosion, China was building militarily. They said that it was to protect themselves, but I wondered. The president informed me that they had not yet had a war and that in Kino they were keeping their armed forces at a minimal level in order to keep the population producing economically and scientifically--because military service is a non-productive, though often essential, appendage to a prosperous economy. Still, she warned, Kino was contemplating a war to stop the air and water pollution of the United States and Europe which was endangering the people and the economy of Kino and the world. The threat had forced the West to rapidly move to cleaning up the global mess that they had spewed on their brothers. The sanctity of nature is too dear to the hearts of the Kinoese to let their world be trashed by their trading partners.

While our conversation filled and flooded my mind, the food and beverages flowed and filled my innards. Never having experienced a Kinoese banquet, I found the repast to be an Epicurean ecstasy. The first course was a paper wrapped portion of grouse with oriental spices. I ate the whole thing. After thirty years of living on pellets and pills I would eat anything. But that morsel was delicious. To my amazement none of my hosts finished their servings. Next came a crow's nest soup. It sounded horrible but tasted great. I finished my bowl. My hosts each took one or two spoons full. Several courses later I was experiencing my fullness and slowed my intake. I was now following my hosts' example of a single bite per course. By the fortieth course I had not a milliliter of room in my stomach for another fraction of a bite. I would have asked for a doggie bag but we ate him in the 29th course. A hundred courses later the feast was finished. I thought I could not be more miserable--but then the speeches started.

Five hours of speeches droned on about the glory of my return. By the time they asked me to relate some of my experiences I had almost reached senility and practically forgot about my trip. But seriously, my hosts were so gracious and I was so happy to be the honoree at their celebration that I was mesmerized by the occasion. I managed a few words between the projected images of the flight that had been prepared for me by NASA. Shots of my landing on Jupiter seemed to be a highlight for them.

TOUR OF THE AREA

The next day I was privileged to be taken on a grand tour of the city and the surrounding area. The small farms, once tended by the peasants, had expanded into huge agricultural businesses--just as in my country. Much of the farming was hydroponic. Kino's government did not give farm subsidies as they have done in continental Europe, the United Kingdom, the United States, Japan and Korea.

Finally over lunch I had a chance to make some comments and ask Madam Ching some questions.

—"I'm wondering about the economy of Kino. I want to see your laboratories. I want to see some manufacturing. I've seen some hydroponic greenhouses but I want to see what you are doing. Has there been any thought to providing subsidies to their agribusiness or to other businesses? "

"Absolutely not! We sponsor some research, but no profit making activities. We do not to pay people to not produce. We do not pay people too produce things that don't pay for themselves. We think there are several negatives to state subsidies.. For one, the taxpayers are paying big money to big farmers to produce things that can be produced much more cheaply in undeveloped nations. I have heard that Switzerland pays extremely high subsidies. Why not just open more ski resorts and train the farmers to teach skiing, or make fondue? The European Union often pays a half billion euros to wine producers during poor growing years which seems to be about every other year. Meanwhile 15 to 20% more wine is being produced in the world than can be sold. Norway pays big subsidies for farms with only one or two growing seasons out of four. But I guess they need the farmers' tractors in the winter to plow the snow away from the roads—so they don't want the farmers going into the information technology businesses.

"In the U.S., the last I heard, the over 20 billion dollars a year of subsidies is nearly 25% of the total farm income. While it reduces the need for the products of the farmers in poorer nations, it keeps the major agri-businessmen in new tractors which they park next to their mansions. Did the American cotton farmers really need $3 billion to produce a product that can be produced more cheaply elsewhere? How many businesses are guaranteed a profit rain or shine? With a good crop farmers make a profit. With a bad crop Uncle Sam fills your piggy bank. And we certainly need farm subsidies for tobacco farmers. Without them the cardiologists and oncologists would need federal subsidies for not having enough pitiful patients lining their waiting rooms.

"The U.S. even pays dead farmers not to farm. A few years ago reporters found that over a billion dollars had been paid to dead farmers because the Department of Agriculture hadn't done the required investigations. One had been dead for over thirty years. So I guess that you are one better than the Scandinavians, you Americans have welfare from cradle to well beyond the grave!

"Perhaps the farm subsidies will end in about ten years as some have suggested but there are a bunch of millionaires who may object. I understand that among the 'farmers' getting a large percent of the more than 50 billion dollars a year are the Queen of England, Prince Charles, the heirs to the WalMart fortune, David Rockefeller and Ted Turner. God knows they need the money!

"The subsidies paid in your rich countries are essential to keep poor countries poor. They allow the farmers in the developed countries to undersell farmers whose countries can't afford to subsidize them. Developing countries argue that government support for US and EU farmers enables those countries to offload produce at artificially low prices, often below the cost of production. Obviously this means unfair competition for producers in poor countries. So the taxpayers may get back a very small part of the taxes they pay for farm subsidies in cheaper steaks or strawberries. And the non-taxpaying food stamp recipients get a discount on what they buy.

"World cotton prices have never been lower but American cotton farmers earn nearly twice as much for their crops because of the subsidies. And the subsidies have been increased because of the falling prices. America's twenty thousand cotton farmers average $5.000 a day each in subsidies. Because of the money in subsidies, more cotton is being raised, even though it isn't needed. Meanwhile sub-Saharan African countries are losing hundreds of millions of dollars a year in lost cotton income. Is this free enterprise a work? Is this the object of globalization?

"The richest of the royalty pick up their share of the farm subsidies. Queen Elizabeth receives well over a million dollars a year, Prince Charles nearly half a million. Other royals receive hefty subsidies for farms that they have inherited from their royal forebears. But the royalty of the rich also pick up their share. The richest man in the UK picks up about a half million dollars from the British taxpayers while Ted Turner and David Rockefeller were also reported to be plowing their fields in their designer jeans—while raking in farm subsidies.

"In the United States if you own land that was once farmed you can generally get a government handout. About $200,000,000 a year goes to people who don't farm. Some make nearly a half a million dollars a year for owning land that was once farmed. Using laws that were originally aimed at eliminating farm subsidies, the amount of money now paid out is higher than when it was given for farming. The amount is now high enough that large land owners who rented farmland are evicting their renters because they can make more money by not farming or renting. So tenant farmers have lost their jobs. In Texas rice farming has decreased by 60% under the new laws. But property owners can turn an extra profit by using their land for non-farming activities such as growing timber or grazing cattle. Much of this is because the federal government's definition of farming does not require that one actually farms. Sounds like Humpty Dumpty's view that a word means what I want it to mean.

"What started in the Depression era as a subsidy to help farmers survive, now hands out $25 billion to farmers and non-farmers even during profitable farming years. The amount spent is far more than is spent on welfare payments. As often happens, temporary or transitional payments often become permanent. There have been other effects also. Farmland prices have increased because they carry the guaranteed government payments with them. Because the non-farmed land is assessed as farmland, the local tax base is reduced so the rich owners pay much less in property taxes. It is so profitable to not farm that real farming is decreasing.

"The realities of politics in a democratic-republic is that to get the necessary votes for a measure you may have to take into consideration special interest groups like farmers, unions or businesses. There is also the political consideration to make a state become beholden to the political party that gives it the most money. So you wouldn't expect politicians to let this sacred cow go un-milked. Consequently a large number of gentlemen farmers line up at the same taxpayer feed trough. If you think that this only happens in the West, just check out Japan's generosity to dairy farmers. It's nearly three times as generous as Uncle Sam!

"When President Bush asked for $120 billion to continue the war in Iraq, Democrats added $3.7 billion to the bill for their pork barrel interests. Representative Bishop from Georgia, a member of the Appropriations Committee, inserted $74 million to cover storage costs for peanuts. Peanut growers had contributed over $35,000 to his campaigns. Representative Farr of California added a $25 million subsidy for spinach growers who hadn't protected their crops from the *e coli* bacterium which was a problem for consumers. They therefore lost money. The growers had donated over $30,000 to his campaigns. And so it goes in our republic, where lobbyists tilt the wheels of progress so that the governmental financial cart always follows the road to the *casa de cash.*

"As you might imagine, being a citizen of the "real" world, it's the big guys that rake in most of the dough. But then they are the bigger contributors to the political races. We're talking about tens of millions to hundreds of millions of dollars a year to the major players in agribusiness. The big guys get about 80% of all of the subsidies. I've rambled on, but I wanted to set the stage of your approach to farming."

—"As in all countries, when sufficient food is raised, other economic, artistic, and philosophic activities can commence. An agricultural surplus is the essential for every true civilization. As in the West, our machinery and robots now do the work that the peasant and the water buffalo used to do. So we don't offer farm subsidies. The farmers produce food and our free market economy sets the prices. We pay more in our markets than you do, but our total cost for food is less because our taxes don't subsidize the food production. This is a very different approach than yours. Forty percent of the EU's budget, $75 billion, goes to food subsidies. Why not just charge the consumers for their food and reduce their taxes? Our food prices are up, as are yours, as more farm land is used for biofuels and fertilizer and transportation costs are up."

THE HISTORY OF CHINA

Madam Ching was particularly proud of China's rich and tumultuous history. She gushed, in an uncharacteristically Western pronouncement that:

"Long before the great teachers Lao Tzu and Confucius, long before Agamemnon attacked Troy, long before Abraham and Sarah—China is. As with every living organism, there are ups and downs, fits and starts, ebbs and flows. China was victimized throughout the Twentieth

Century. No nation in history has risen from the bottom to the top as quickly as has China. It's getting it right. And as former party leader Deng Xiaoping said 'to get right is glorious.'

"It's not to the top yet but it has shed the anchor of the teeming rabble through its population foresight, and it has risen to the surface. Everyone knows there are problems. There is a big gap between rich and poor. Civil liberties are barely surfacing. One party rule has many drawbacks. But the strong central government has made some good decisions, which outnumber its errors. It is unquestionably moving forward at a speed no other large country can match."

I needed to find out more about China and how Kino fit in to the futuristic expanding puzzle. As I evaluated and internalized Madam Ching's words I remember that when I was in elementary school I was aware of the fact that China had a population out of control with a subsistence economy not able to keep up with the expanding population. The nuns continually reminded us of 'the poor starving children of China.' I also knew that 20 years before I had left on my voyage that the country had begun a plan to limit every family to only one child. Deng Xiaoping was in charge in 1980 when the one child policy was initiated. Amid much grumbling, that plan had been effected and the population began to level off. In 2006 the decision was made to continue the policy.

It is projected that by 2050 China's economy will be the biggest in the world. It is currently growing 3 times faster than that of the USA. It is growing at nearly 7% per year. It has had to overcome its banking and educational problems in order to become a truly great economy—and it has done these rapidly. Its currency increases in value. Its educational system is growing effectively. And the president wanted me to know that Kino was helping to show China the way.

The drop in China's population has been unequaled in a peacetime world. While some countries have been nearly annihilated by the ravages of revolution or war, by the devastation of pandemic diseases such as the Black Death and the AIDS virus, or by the painful and pitiful deaths due to famine

-- a state directed peacetime drop in population such as I have seen here in Kino, and is evident in China, has no modern historical equivalent.

While the warriors of ancient Sparta may have challenged their newborns to test the elements on the barren hillside, thereby allowing for only the strongest to survive, no other example comes to mind in which a society's population has been so radically controlled.

And so Kino, along with China, is on its way to being one of the great civilizations of history. And all because it chose to limit its population and allow for the maximal development of its citizens and its other natural resources. Their position is that it is not so important to reflect on the past but to control the future. This they are doing. They have that old fashioned idea that leaders should lead a country into the future. In most modern democracies the elected leaders follow the loudest voices in the crowd. They soothe their concerns. They pragmatically 'lead' with only the present in mind—with the next election being the only vision in their myopic values.

The area encompassing modern China has been active for over 5000 years. But since it was unified in 221 B.C., the supposedly unified country has been plagued by warring areas. The Communists put a stop to this by unifying the country, killing the protestors, developing economic plans and looking for solutions that would fit it into the technological world as it became more globally involved.

With the speed of communication in the world during the last thirty years it is difficult to hide the truth from the people. Whether it was the inefficiency of Soviet economic policies, the desire for a better life by the Chinese or the realities of the ill-conceived war in Iraq for the Americans and British—it doesn't take long for the truth to be known. The ruling group whether Communists, Democrats, Tories, Republicans or Labour has to adjust to the realities of the world and the realistic possibilities for the people. So if the rulers want to stay in power, they must adjust or bust.

The Chinese Communists did this. While keeping a tight thumb on dissent, they opened their vast pool of labor to the capitalists. They allowed some religion, but made certain that Beijing, not Rome, Tibet or America, was in control. So the Communist government became an advocate of capitalism to survive. It may sound strange but even the young capitalists are members of the Communist Party. It doesn't really matter what you call it, as long as it works.

ECONOMICS

China's income gap provokes some alarm. Under Mao the Communist government took the land and property of the rich so that incomes could be leveled under state control. But while state run businesses are losing money the allowed free enterprise is making great amounts of money. As is generally true, state run businesses tend to be inefficient. The profit motive and the real chance of business failure keep the private entrepreneurs on their toes. It reminds me of a state run shoe factory in the Soviet Union that exceeded its quota in shoe manufacture, but all the shoes were for left feet. Would an entrepreneur have allowed this to happen?

So soon the top 20% of the population made 50% of the money. Fifteen years ago the bottom 20% of the population made about 5% of the money. Today the minimum wages have increased that considerably. The lowest economic groups are no longer earning at a Third World rate of a dollar a day. They are out of the poverty levels and they are moving up the economic ladder quickly. More need for workers combined with more jobs has driven wages way up. This, then, has driven the price of their exports up.

13

The Chinese yuppies are following the American way of pursuing money and the things it can bring—less free time but more material accoutrements. The rich have a huge amount of money to spend on such things as French perfume, designer clothes, and high tech computers. The young children of prosperous Chinese have been spoiled by the unlimited supply of money from their rich parents. Just like in the US, it often happens that when a person hasn't earned something he doesn't appreciate it and he stays an emotionally selfish person. There is no sense of responsibility. This runs exactly counter to the rules Confucius found to be necessary for an orderly society. Without a sense of order and some feeling of duty and responsibility you have anarchy, not society. Madam Ching informed me that in Kino they work to insure that the valuable traditions of the past are honored and adhered to. Of course those that are counter to developing a cooperating democracy we minimize or forget.

In the late 90s in China the entrepreneurial types often pirated clothes, music, films. They had decided to beat free enterprise at its own game. The government looked the other way as long as it didn't cost them anything. Motorola taught them how to make phones, then some Chinese made them cheaper and took many of the markets. This has led to foreign firms keeping their research away from the natives. So the Chinese had to become part of the established world economy. If you want to partake in the spoils of globalization, you had better follow the rules of the 'globalizers.' And they don't take kindly to patent or copyright infringements.

But most Chinese are relatively poor—some extremely poor. This has forced many young girls into prostitution—because it is harder for women to find and keep jobs than it is for men. This has forged questions of values—the self centered values of the West are conflicting with the societal values espoused by the earlier Communists and the traditional societal values of Confucius. What should be the principles of fairness and justice for their society. Should there be the economic equality that Marx desired? But such equality has only been found in the monasteries and convents of the Christians and Buddhists.

--"In the West, laws and unions have given the workers more money, but the Communist government has not yet done this. First there must be work, then there must be more benefits from that work. In Kino we have had the financial blessings of China and have increased the real wages, including retirement and health care benefits. China will follow us after its first goal of full employment is met. They have already started with free tuition and books and with a small bit of old age pensions.

"Of course the workers want more and faster benefits from their labor. But the evolution of economic benefits must come from the top down. The Soviet Union tried a more equalitarian distribution of wages. It didn't work.

"We were able to speed up the process here in Kino because of the extra money given us and the fact that our labor force was more intellectual. Hand labor and factory labor is just not that valuable when there are plenty of hands available to do the work. Realistically there is a 'quality' of labor that has to be recognized. A person with a vision, who has the necessary knowledge and a work ethic, is more valuable than someone who can merely clean up a hotel room. Just about anyone can do that. But how many people have the expertise to design a fuel-efficient auto engine, an automobile that runs on solar power, or the knowledge necessary develop a Microsoft or a Google? In Western free enterprise a person's vision and ability is honored financially. When such concepts are developed, the financial rewards will either trickle or flood down. People who are academically prepared and have shown that they can perform will be in great demand. Some of the rewards are financial, others are in acquiring status, and still others in job satisfaction. We think that each of these potential rewards is worth pursuing. Seeking rewards just because you are a human being does not fit in our system. You must be a valuable part of the system—making contributions.

"Mao's vision tended to work to put things on a more equal footing. In Kino we believe that real equality of opportunity must start with effective parenting, this is followed by equal educational opportunity that is available without charge throughout one's lifetime. Then we expect the person to produce, as a researcher, policeman, teacher, business person, et cetera. And when a person is producing effectively that real progress must be rewarded.

"Our societal fundamentals are somewhat similar to the ideas of Ashley Montagu and Sigmund Freud who said that to be a useful citizen a person must be able to love and work. The love input begins with choosing parents who are able to love. We continue children's nurturing in schools by following your American pattern of teaching children to take turns. They must realize that each person is important at an early age. Then the schools teach the responsibility to be productive. And, of course, the major effort of the schools is the help to develop the tools that civilization has found to be essential, along with the knowledge and skills necessary to compete and produce in this modern ever-changing world. So our education system emphasizes logical development through studying philosophy and logic. We study and practice physical activity as part of the general knowledge of mental and physical health. We study the psychological and social sciences, particularly history. And we study mathematics and the natural sciences. Academic achievement is recognized and rewarded.

"Let me contrast our education model with China's. We have followed China's educational system to some degree but have increased the availability and lessened the cost. As you probably know, education is free in China up to nine years of education. Primary school goes to the sixth grade. Middle school goes to the ninth grade. The state pays for tuition and books at these levels. Students go to school generally from about 7 AM to 4 PM and often to Saturday classes. Students going to a three-year high school must pay tuition and buy the books. And if the school is a long way from home they must board there. Then university costs are quite low by American standards. University education can be 4 to 6 years.

"In Kino all of our education is free. We can't afford yet to give every university student a scholarship as they do in Norway, but we are getting closer. Our primary schools are similar to China's but we tried to get away from the rote memory that they use as a primary pedagogic tool. We want our students to be able to solve problems. Of course you can't solve problems unless you have some knowledge. We are using robots to teach many of the courses, like the robots that teach English in South Korea. We also use video games as a way of teaching math and science. We also use part of the day for physical education activities – – to develop physical fitness and to learn sports. Naturally English is a major subject from the first grade.

"In middle school we have afternoon sports after our classes dismiss at 4 PM. We have a number of options for afterschool activities. We have taken a page from the Soviet Union's approach with their Young Pioneer Palaces. We don't have Young Pioneers in our country but the gigantic buildings that the Soviets had for free time education were exceptional. Students could choose to learn ballet, gymnastics, astronomy, advanced physics, tailoring, advanced mathematics, languages, soccer, competitive swimming or track and field, basketball, world history or any number of other valuable skills.

"At the university level tuition and books are free and room and board are inexpensive. But we must insist that the students have part-time jobs – – often at the university. Sometimes they work in businesses that are related to their university major studies. We also require some of your American MOOC courses. They are outstanding and usually free. We also bring in professors from your country and Canada as well as Europe when they are on sabbatical leaves or retired.

"We realize that education is more than transferring knowledge—students must experience people who can excite them personally and professionally. Knowledge is only a part of education—the development of values that provide lifelong commitment to advancing our society, developing a loving family and the advancing of sound academic knowledge are all essential to an educated person. The pursuit of financial gluttony is something that separates our society from most of yours.

"We emphasize honesty as essential in a society based on social values. Criminal behavior is severely punished. Organized crime that is so evident in many countries has not gained a foothold here. Petty crime is also severely punished. So we attack dishonesty through both punishment and through social disapproval.. We guard against the anti-social groups that might applaud crime, such as your youth gangs and mafias. But our experience is that our parenting licensing, with its emphasis on effectively loving our children, is the key to social awareness and concern for others. There is no question that criminality in your country is largely caused by unprepared, unloving and incompetent parents.

"One of our biggest problems when we started this province was in making government workers honest. Graft seems to be a way of life in most societies, especially the traditionally poorer states. It is still prevalent in China, but has been wiped out here. We are now rated with Finland as the most graft-free countries."

CORRUPTION

"Selfishness is a natural psychological imperative. You can see why it is so prevalent in most societies. In developing countries there is certainly the need for food--and money. But the desire for money leads most people into a reckless pursuit of wealth for its own sake. So often we see wealth as power – – and power is the nearly universal aphrodisiac. The drive for money can be met within the law or outside of the law. We find it commonly in graft within bureaucracies and businesses. Cross my palm with silver and I will make certain that you get to the head of the line, whether you want medical care, a marriage license or a building approval.

"The OECD is currently prosecuting a number of cases for bribery in its membership. Both France and Turkey are major culprits in this international scandal.(1)

"This nearly universal practice is counterproductive to good government. But one of the greatest evils is in the organized crime rings that are present in most societies. The Italian Mafia, the Japanese Yakusa, the Russian "mafia", the street gangs like the Bloods and Crips, and even the nominally religious Taliban and Islamic State. It is not only those that seek money and power but those who want to make society according to their own selfish ideas. The Taliban and IS use violence and drug money to advance their cause. And in the case of the Islamic State, they take over oil production as a means of finance. Boku Haram is another such group.

"The second great financial evil is organized religion. By eliminating religion we can minimize the illegal activities of many of these religious groups. When Karl Marx said that "religion is the opiate of the people" he was right on track. Telling people that the ideal society will be experienced after they die is not the best way to develop a society here and now. Just look at past. Religious hierarchies controlled the Christians in Europe and the Muslims in the Middle East and North Africa. They still do it in your country with their massive tax breaks for the huge amounts of land that are owned by religions, particularly the Catholics and the Mormons. Your citizens have to pay higher taxes and borrow more from China to support those religions and their quest for more money and more power. I don't know if the religions in America are worse than the mafias and gangs that you have. Actually they **are** probably worse in terms of stealing from the citizens. It makes me laugh when I see the reverence you Americans pay to the people whom you see as holy just because they say they represent an unknowable spirit whose existence can never be proven. Very primitive!

"I would also call your tax avoiding corporation corrupt. In America many of your largest companies pay no tax at all. With all the deductions that lobbyists have had written into the laws, everything is deductible – – from salaries and health benefits to depreciation on everything that moves or doesn't move. So America's high tax rate on corporations, the world's highest at 39%, is laughable.

"With your single focus on money, your major corporations move their companies around like pieces on a chessboard. Whatever country will give them the lowest tax rate is where they will land.

"Certainly no government is as legally corrupt as yours. Allowing lobbyists as representatives of businesses and other organizations to bribe your legislators would be a definite crime in most countries. But your legislators have made it legal in the US. In China and here in Kino such activities would be major crimes carrying a minimum penalty of 25 years, and in some cases, capital punishment. Then your Republican appointed Supreme Court in 2010 in the case Citizens United v. Federal Election Commission, extended a long held principle that in many ways a corporation can be treated as a person, even though they had to overturn or partially overturn other Supreme Court decisions and had to refute the opinions of prior respected judges like Hugo Black and William O. Douglas who had held that corporate personhood was not an 'all or nothing' principle. They allowed corporations to fund election campaigns. In our country or Chia you would all be jailed.

YOUR UNQUESTIONED PURSUIT OF WEALTH

"It surprises me that in your supposedly religious country you don't understand that 'you can't take it with you.' Your country is getting richer but few of the people feel it.

"What happened to the sermon on the Mount and the idea that it is harder for rich man to enter the kingdom of heaven than it is for a camel to pass to the eye of the needle. Or what about' the meek shall inherit the earth.' If you are religious you certainly don't follow any principles of

Christianity. Even your major preachers want bigger amphitheaters in which to kill the Satanic gladiators' The Chrystal Cathedral in Orange County California and the First Baptist Dallas in Texas come to mind.

Your Tea Party patriots criticize our socialistic welfare state ideas, without understanding what socialism is. They want their Social Security, which is socialistic because' it is from each according to his ability to each according to his work." And they want their Medicare, which is communistic 'from each according to his ability to each according to his needs.' Your people just don't think, at least it seems to be true for the majority of your electorate. It seems to us that having a happy population is far more important than having low taxes."

"Points well taken. With the Maoist revolution, a strong state was created, but society was weakened, I think. There is no question that the strong central government and the unity of purpose you have had with your Constitution enabled China to progress. But of course it could not have progressed without intelligent leadership. It was the foreword thinking of the leaders that reduced the population increases and led the country effectively into the modern age.

It was evident that people had moved to where manufacturing could be accomplished. This had already started before my voyage, and businesses of the West had flocked to Kino to take advantage of their relatively low wages and their high quality products. The strong work ethic of the Kinoese, stimulated by the opportunity for monetary rewards their pride in accomplishment had catapulted their economy--which sped like a spaceship to a level never before seen in the history of business.

While much of the technological know-how was learned or bought from the United States and Western Europe, the post-socialist Chinese and Kinoese left their countries to learn at the great universities of the world, today many great universities are here. Cutting edge research in medicine, genetics, engineering and even the humanities have made the universities of Kino the envy of every other country. And probably its greatest academic achievement is that it has only one law school, and, just as in the U.S., it seldom attracts top students. Legal cases are decided primarily through computer programs. Since there is no monetary incentive to sue rich companies it is not done. It is the job of the government to legislate away problem industries. Accident and divorce settlements, harassment charges, contract issues and employment problems are all programmed into the computers that evaluate the application of laws for the society. The legal system is founded on the simpler Napoleonic law which is based on the actual statutes rather than on the Common Law that has given Englishmen and Americans so many ways to get around the statutes enacted by their legislatures.

The president reminded me that "Confucius said that the essentials of good government are sufficient food, sufficient armament and the confidence of the people. It is the confidence of the people that is primary. 'Rotten wood may not be carved, nor can a wall be plastered with manure.'(2)   I wondered where are Kino and China in terms of coping with today's economic and ethical problems? Madam Ching filled me in saying that:

--"There have been some benefits from globalization. There certainly is more money in our country.   As the Chinese population becomes richer it buys more cars and oil, more electronics products, uses more water, pollutes more air and does all of the same negative things that the advanced economies of the U.S., Japan, Korea and Europe do. When the Chinese people have as many cars per capita as you do in the U.S.A. it would require 80 million barrels of oil per day to run them. But the world production of oil is only 64 million barrels a day and the available reserves are not increasing. There is a finite supply of oil. So we use solar power.

"The low economic end of the Chinese society, and even people higher up the money mountain often turn to drugs for solace. Many youth have become heroine addicts. Heroin addiction in many parts of the country help in fueling the AIDS crisis. Over 20 million are now infected through freer sex and contaminated needles.

"Drugs have been a long term problem in China with opium apparently being brought to us in the 7th and 8th centuries by the Arabs, then by the British in the 18th Century, there has been a long history of opiate use. And the government has always fought bitterly against it. We lost the opium wars to the British so we were forced to allow opium imports. Under the Communists drug use took a big drop. But now there is some money to buy oneself out of unhappiness and powerlessness, so the false hope of psychoactive chemicals has reappeared, particularly among the young. The Chinese government has executed a number or drug dealers and importers, but the problem persists. Recently alcohol has made a great leap forward. Wine is now even being cultivated in China—but not here in Kino. We discourage the use of any drugs.

"In Kino we have had little problem with psychoactive drugs. Part of the education required for parent licensing deals with drug education. Why people use them. How to see the symptoms of drug use. And mainly how to be loving parents. We think that is the major key—loving children and educating them. We believe that if children feel good about themselves as children and youth they won't have the need to escape their reality. Then if we educate them about the many negative consequences of drug use, they will not have the inclination to experiment.

"We also have mandatory blood tests throughout the year in schools and work places. We test primarily for diseases and drug use. We want to catch any potential problem for an individual and for the society while it is in its infancy. It is much more difficult to solve a mature addiction or a pandemic disease.

"In Kino the social inequities found in China have been largely eliminated. Women and men have equal opportunities for education, jobs and pay. There is therefore no need for aborting female fetuses.

"There is still the official need to keep population controlled. While population reduction would have been undesirable in an agricultural country, it is highly desirable in a developing technological country. With fewer people a greater percentage of the youth can be highly educated. Automated factories produced more goods which resulted in more money for the relatively fewer people in our society. As the per capita income grew the standards of living became increasingly higher.

"It was not long before we had surpassed both China and your country, where your national debt has engulfed and hobbled your 'huddled masses' while you taxed your workers to pay for the non-producers. Kino has blended the ethical concerns and the industriousness of our Chinese traditions with a free thinking scientific method that it has applied to directing our society. While we have some democratic tendencies, enough to keep the people happy by thinking that they are in control, we also have a strong central government which has the power to enforce traditional ethical beliefs as laws and to develop the necessary societal directions which, while sometimes suppressing what you call freedoms, assured a better life for the future of our citizens and their children.

"In Kino the government annually determines how many babies are needed for that year. We then issue that many licenses to the highest qualified potential parents. We sometimes allow for more licenses than we actually need, especially if particularly effective parents apply. Generally, though, we want to reduce our population.

"As other developed countries have found, as women move up the economic ladder they often choose their vocation to the exclusion of having children. For some, being a brain surgeon or a senator, far outweighs the expected joys of parenthood—and it certainly reduces the responsibilities. For those who want both we have inexpensive child care or we can split jobs so that the child's caretaker, whether it be the father or the mother, can do both. Once the child is in school most of the problems are over—assuming that the parent works a normal 7 to 9 hour day.

"Being an effective parent is essential to having intelligent and mentally stable citizens. So we assign a monetary value to caretaking and factor that into the state's cost of progressing socially and economically.

"China was an innovator millennia ago. But as the centuries passed the burden of overpopulation and wars brought it to a subsistence economy. Communism held back the natural intelligence and industriousness of the Chinese people. It moved toward superpower status only at the turn of this millennium. Still with over a billion people it was difficult to get into gear. The central government therefore cut our province loose from our parent country so we were free to experiment and prosper, hoping that we could find a better and quicker way for the whole country of China to move."

-- "Madam Ching, while my main concern is your population control strategy, I'd like to know some more about other areas of the economic and social aspects of your country and how they compare and contrast with both China and the West. Let's start with health. As a former professor of health education I am certainly interested in this area."

HEALTH CONCERNS

-- "We have looked at some of China's problems, and problems from the rest of the world and tried to eliminate them. For example, China has 320 million smokers. 90% of adult males smoke. That's about twice the world's rate. Smoking now accounts for one in 8 deaths in China but will rise to 1 in 3 by 2050 if the current trends continue. In China this has significantly increased health care costs. Nearly 60% of doctors smoke, most people still don't know the risks of lung and other cancers or the major killer from smoking-- heart disease. It is true that the antioxidants in green tea seem to reduce some of the negative effects of smoking. So we may not have quite as many problems from smoking as you do in the West.

"However in Kino we have very high taxes on tobacco and we require a license to use tobacco products. The terms of that license are that smoking related problems will not be covered by the national health insurance. So the various cancers that are tobacco related, such as lung and mouth cancers, emphysema, high cholesterol or high blood pressure related heart problems are not covered by the regular state supplied insurance. But people can purchase additional insurance for smoking related diseases. Of course it is quite expensive.

"We begin our tobacco, alcohol and other drug education programs in the first year of school. We also have television ads against smoking and we do not allow actors to smoke on screen for TV or movie programs. Any film that shows a person smoking is not allowed in our country. Film producers know this so they either cut or re-do the scenes with tobacco in them. We are a large market for films so we command respect and compliance by the film producers.

"In our education we also show the moral decadence of smoking and how it is a harmful, but simple, way for people to soothe their inferiority complexes. Just look at the way your advertising is geared to being important, sensual and powerful. Whether it is the macho Marlboro man or the successful woman in the Virginia Slims ads, tobacco advertising is geared to showing that you can be better than you are just by lighting up. But no sense spending time on the psychology behind it because I know you will go much more in depth into motivations when you talk with Chuck Chan in Singaling.

"Suffice to say that no intelligent person would ever smoke, unless somehow earlier addicted. After all, tobacco addiction is rated as the most difficult or the second most difficult drug from which to withdraw. The difficulty stems to a large degree from the fact that while most drugs give either an upper or a downer effect, tobacco gives both. It stimulates like adrenaline and it calms by acting like the calming neurotransmitter acetylcholine. So when you withdraw from the drug you have both the crashing effect of an upper drug like cocaine or methamphetamine and the hyper-excitability of a heroin type downer. Of course the withdrawals are not nearly as severe as withdrawing from cocaine or heroin, but they occur together so you have dual and opposite nervous system reactions simultaneously.

"A new international study confirms that exposure to cigarette smoke before and after birth impairs the lung function of the child. Parental smoking remains a serious public health issue after the birth of the child also. Therefore smoking automatically eliminates one from obtaining a license to parent in Kino. It is not only the lung function that is affected, but a large percentage of attention deficit disorders seem to be smoking related.

"There are over a hundred chemicals in tobacco smoke. One of the most harmful is carbon monoxide which, as you know, makes the blood less efficient by cutting down on oxygen transportation. This can potentially reduce the optimal development of all body organs.

"While the negative effects of smoking on an infant begin during pregnancy, the negative effects continue for the child or adult while living with the smoker. The smoking by an expectant mother is a highly negative factor for the infant, but the second hand smoke of an expectant father begins its damage to the unborn infant due to the effects of carbon monoxide and other tobacco chemicals. That second hand smoke from the father or mother continues to be a negative for the child. For that reason smoking is not allowed in a household if parents are to be licensed to have a child."

"It seems that the developing body may be susceptible to different toxins at different stages of development. In animal studies, alcohol damages an embryo within the first 4 days after conception. As you know alcohol can kill nerve cells in adults, so you can imagine what it can do to a developing embryo or fetus. It and other drug use are also related to faulty nervous system development and to related neurological problems. So alcohol use is forbidden for licensed parents beginning a month before they can attempt to conceive.

"Our bodies are susceptible to so many toxins. For example the polycyclic aromatic hydrocarbons or PAHs that come from smoke like tobacco smoke, wood burning and barbequing smoke and the meat barbequed can harm both adults and children. The combination of genetic and environmental problems are responsible for a large number of children's physical and mental problems, so we try to reduce the potential problems through licensing responsible people to have children."

--"How is your health care handled?"

-- "Our health insurance follows the long standing Chinese principle of paying the doctor when you are well but not when you are sick. So our health insurance payments go to the doctors monthly. Those health insurance costs are paid by the people. Every family pays a part. There are discounts for regular effective exercising. Exercise attendance is monitored by the various sport and fitness clubs, or for those who want to exercise alone, like bike riders or surfers, by heart monitor records that are downloaded in people's computers and sent daily to the National Health Registry. Factors such as overweight, cholesterol and other blood measurements are submitted by the doctors after a person's annual physical exam.

"We recognize that regular exercise is more important for one's health than are many drugs and operations. And weight control is essential too. Just look at the heart disease and diabetes rates between our two countries. Our people are trim and active, yours are often obese media mongrels reclining with their trusted companion, the TV's remote control. Of course we have never been addicted to fats as you people have, so we haven't had to go on reduced fat diets. With our traditional Asian diet we were already there.

"Just a few preventive life style changes could reduce your health care bills by 30 to 40%. Your own research shows that half of your deaths were attributed to preventable exposures or behaviors. (3) We see your citizens as looking for pills, gadgets and operations to fill all your mental and physical health needs. Whether it's plastic surgery, psychiatry or pep pills, you search for a better self through science—not self-discipline. That goes against the basic tenets for our people. We believe that we should be0 responsible for ourselves as much as is humanly possible.

"In our society we believe that people should be responsible for themselves and pay for what they need. So while we have nationalized health insurance we don't have socialized medicine in which every person is entitled to care just because he is human. We believe that he must be a responsible human. You can imagine that we keep the national actuaries busy sorting out the increased and decreased risks for every health problem and ascertaining the increased or decreased costs for every individual for every condition. But our 30 years of in depth studying of health and disease gives us the largest continuous study of a population in the world. We've taken your Framingham Study and expanded it by a factor of thousands." Of course since smoking is estimated to kill a billion people this century, maybe it should be encouraged—at least in other countries."

MEDICAL COSTS IN THE U.S.

--"I like your ideas Madam President. But in my country the medical costs increase throughout life and through retirement. Doctors' fees are up, hospital costs are up, prescription drugs costs are up."

--"Don't your lawyers have a part in this?"

--"Yes, a big part. When they sue an effective doctor, whether they win or lose, malpractice insurance rates go up. Naturally this has to be reflected in the doctor's cost of doing business. Then because of the fear of legal actions doctors order every possible test for a condition. This can then be used as a defense should a patient sue. These costs are then reflected in the medical fees paid by the patient, by the insurance company or by the state or the national health insurance coverages. Many medical malpractice cases never get to court. They are settled out of court because the defending lawyers have no idea as to what a jury will award. And by settling the lawyer gets his 30 to 40% fee easily. Juries don't always concern themselves with the facts. But that can be expected because people are more psychological than logical. So if a lawyer is an effective psychologist, the jury can be worked to think in terms of sympathy for the plaintiff rather than justice and can award an undeserving victim millions. It's a legal lottery.

"If the doctor had a jury of his peers, all with M.D. degrees, more cases would go to court and the suing lawyers would find that such suits were not profitable for them to pursue. But since juries are generally made up of poorer citizens, often with minimal educations, the lawyers know they can get settlements based on appeals to emotions. In our court system emotional appeals usually trump the facts. And for lawyers it is about winning and making money—not justice. Do you have such legal problems in Kino?"

KINO'S LEGAL APPROACH

--"No. We use a computerized legal approach. It does the analysis of facts computed against the laws. We don't have lawyers making 35 to 40% contingency fees on any settlement. It keeps our medical bills down. And it keeps the awards in all lawsuits fair. As many countries have done, we eliminated juries long ago."

PRESCRIPTION DRUGS

--"In America there's another factor that keeps our medical costs up. American consumers pay a good part of the research costs of new drugs. When pharmaceutical companies bid for a whole country, as they do in countries with socialized medicine, they come in with low prices. As a result drugs cost less in most other countries. If you compare the cost of identical drugs in the U.S. with the costs in Mexico, Spain, Greece or any other country, you find the U.S. is much higher."

--"In Kino we don't have much of a pharmaceutical industry here so we must rely on other countries to develop and test their drugs. We believe that we should share in that development cost as part of the drug expense. But we don't want to share in the marketing costs. In your country the doctors' offices may have more drug company representatives in their waiting rooms than they have patients. To the degree that they are informing doctors, we think that is OK. But to the degree that they are influencing doctors to use equal or inferior drugs, we think that is uncalled for.

"We also have a rule that we will not accept research articles from doctors who are accepting money from drug companies. Our medical journals accept only untainted research. We do allow the pharmaceutical companies to cooperate on drug reports for each disease condition. However, the research they present must be unbiased. If we find untruthful statements in a report, that company's drugs are not allowed to be sold in our country for five years. The reports vary with the disease. So if the report is on prostate cancer, all drug companies are invited to submit their drug information regarding prevention and cure. Our panel of experts thoroughly examines all of the research used to back up the claims. We pay the expert panel for their time. The report is then available to any of our physicians who request it. We don't allow media advertising by pharmaceutical companies in which they attempt to influence the potential patients. We let the medical experts, not the patients, determine the need for a drug.

"Just look at the ridiculous way your government handled the Medicare drug bill a few years ago. Many low income people who had been getting their drugs free from the pharmaceutical companies were prohibited from doing so. They had to make additional payments into the national coffers for drugs and the drug companies were guaranteed top dollar on the sales because the law specifically prohibited Medicare from bargaining with them for lower prices. Yet all other countries and some U.S. agencies, like the Veterans Health Administration and the Defense Department were doing just that.

"We want to be fair to the pharmaceutical companies, but we're not going to play Daddy Warbucks to their Orphan Annie! A major difference between our country and yours is that we look out for the good of the whole society first, then we consider the desires of the citizens. We don't allow lobbyists to influence our decisions.

DEMOCRACY AND----WESTERN STYLE TEENAGERS-DRUGS, CLOTHES, SEX

"China has been effective economically and is moving slowly towards a Western style of thinking, which many call democracy. Unhappily the worst aspects of your democracy—the self centered aspect—are the first things that attract people's attention. It allowed the young in China to emulate their Western cousins—peroxided California blonds, rave parties, gratuitous uncaring and unprotected sex, and the selfishness that accompanies the promise of freedom.

'But self-centeredness is not the essential of democracy. It is instead the basis for a lack of responsibility—for license! It is pure democracy to vote your self centered interests. But this is a far cry from the visions of an enlightened democracy for all the people. Whether we look at the ancient Athenians' democracy only for the male citizens, or the thinkers of the Enlightenment who envisioned a broader seat of power, they wanted a political power of educated, wise and socially conscious citizens. Wise political philosophers expected that the electorate's decisions would evolve heavenward, lifting the population with them. But as psychologists might well have predicted, selfishness is more likely to be the immediate goal of those who can't see past today. Self interest is expected, but enlightened self interest should be the goal.

"We see that self interest, particularly in China. While there is much poverty, the Chinese yuppies are buying cars and apartments, furniture and toys. Their one child is pampered. They are following the American way of pursuing money and the things it can bring—less time but more goodies. An advanced political democracy hasn't yet arrived in China. They don't have the free speech to criticize their leaders or accuse them of crimes. They are still in a soviet style government in which keeping order is primary. You can only do what the government allows. Kino is different.

"In Kino we are trying to bring all of our citizens to a much higher level of democracy. As Confucius said, we must apply the fundamentals. Once the fundamentals are there, the system comes into being.' (4) The more mature democrats realize that there has to be an element of love, of caring for others, because we are all in this together. This is what allows a democratic society to evolve toward the 'good.' Without this altruistic evolution we stay in the infantile world of greed and loneliness. And here is where we breed the mafias, the drug addicts, the drunk drivers and the rapists --whose only thoughts are for themselves and their concern with 'pleasure now.' If the society is to be better we must vote and behave with enlightened self-interest, with a broader societal perspective, with a higher concept of 'the GOOD.'

"Again we look to Confucius who saw that it is not laws and punishment that are most effective in making citizens comply with the ethics of the society, but rather the inward compulsion to do right and to avoid shame. As he said 'If people are kept in a system by administration and are treated as equals in the manner of punishment, they may succeed in doing no wrong, but they will also feel no sense of shame. On the other hand if they are kept in the system by 'excellence' and are treated as equals before the laws, they will reform themselves through a sense of shame.' (5)

"In a democratic vote the people think they are getting what they want, what's good for them, but politically astute people, which often includes the chief elected officers and the members of the legislatures, can manipulate the people and establish what amounts to a near totalitarian government. Just look at what happened in the early years of this century in your country. Lies and 'spin' got a government elected that took you to war, significantly increased your national debt, increased the price of oil by decreasing the value of your dollar by half, spied on innocent citizens, and gave major tax breaks to the rich. Your policies and actions developed an incredible dislike and even hatred from both your international friends and enemies. Your leaders' masterful use of propaganda and other psychological techniques controlled your electorate. Your leaders invoked fear of both real and imaginary enemies. They called on your honor to defend democracy and to spread it. And they did this the full blessings and support of God. You Americans have been the most militant pacifists in the history of the world.

"It is our belief that democracy, as it is practiced, is not guaranteed to be the ultimate form of government. It can be effective but it is not guaranteed. A benevolent dictatorship can certainly be preferable. For any government to work it must place the good of the country foremost. Not necessarily in the immediate future but for the long term. As Aristotle said "It is harder to preserve than to found a democracy." (6)

OUR ONE CHILD POLICY

--"Madam Ching, that is all very interesting. But can you now to fill me in on the details of the 'one child' policy and its progress. You know that is a burning interest of mine."

--"Well Commander, China's population in 1950 was about 600 million, by 2005 it had more than doubled to 1.3 billion in spite of its drastic population control methods. Now in 2020 it is 1.5 billion. The female fertility rate was reduced from nearly six children per woman in 1970 to 1.7, and is now dropping closer to the European rates.(7) It is still higher than Denmark, Greece, Italy and Germany. It is definitely not 1.0, like so many people think!

"Even though the population actually increased by 250 million during the first 25 years of the 'one child' policy it resulted in 400 million fewer births than there would have been without the policy. This meant 400 million fewer mouths to feed and 400 million fewer to educate. That 400 million reduction in births is equivalent to the combined populations of the United States and Mexico. And while the population is still increasing at about 10 million a year, it is slowing. In about 30 more years, by 2050 it should begin reversing

"In your country you have been concerned about 12 million illegal immigrants. What would have been the economic result of having 400 million more babies in a 25 year period. Wouldn't it have had a bit of an effect on your education systems, your health system, your job creation potential, your housing, your electrical power production, your oil needs?"

--"Obviously. I had just never given that any thought. Mexico can't handle its own population problems and won't do anything about it so they call on my country to be humanitarian and take in all who want to come. Many are objecting to the 12 million illegal immigrants. As you say, 400,000,000 would be impossible to handle. We would be a Third World country overnight."

--"And with your partisan politics and archaic religious ideas there is no way for your country to make such changes—even when they are needed.

"Commander, you are well aware of the two obvious problems that have resulted from reducing the population in China. First there is the excess of males to females. Then there is the graying of the population. But whatever the results of the one child policy, it worked well. No historian would expect such a major societal change without some attendant problems. Let's start with the imbalance of the sexes.

CHINA'S IMBALANCE OF SEXES

"In China males were preferred because of their greater earning power, which was essential on the farms and in the cities where pensions had been reduced. Males were needed to care for their parents in their old age. As we all know, throughout history males have generally been preferred as rulers, as teachers, as doctors, and so—as children. The female exceptions of the past like the legendary Queen Eyleuka of Ethiopia in 4500 BCE and Pharaoh Hatshepsut of Egypt --right up through leaders like Cleopatra and Elizabeth, all had gained power through bloodlines. But recently we have had elected leaders like Indira Gandhi, Margaret Thatcher and Angela Merkel. These show that women could and can lead. But it is difficult to lead when you are barefoot and pregnant and have six little mouths to feed. Women's inferior placement was determined more by male physical strength and a lack of contraceptives than by natural talent. Rulers have often been chosen because of their success on the battlefields. Here again women were nearly universally excluded from battle. In the few cases where women were battle leaders it didn't change the status of women. The Trung sisters of Vietnam led a revolt against the Chinese in 40AD. But they lost and committed suicide. Queen Tomyris, taking over from her dead husband, led the battle against the Persians, defeated them and killed King Cyrus in 529 BC. And Joan of Arc was rather successful on the battlefield until she was burned at the stake in 1431 at the age of 19.

"So male children have been traditionally preferred because they are more muscular warriors and quite less likely to get pregnant! But traditions are seldom overcome by intelligence or the recognition of a superior value system. Traditions give our unthinking minds firm foundations in the quicksand of ignorance. And they will eventually sink into oblivion. We needed to change the tradition here in Kino regarding preferences for males. We have eliminated the preference for males and seldom use amniocentesis for sex selection.

"South Korea showed us the way when they reversed their male to female birth ratio from 117 boys per 100 girls in 1990 back to the norm of 105 boys per 100 girls. They did it by outlawing amniocentesis for sex selection, which decreased abortions for female fetuses, and by the government's message that 'one daughter is worth ten sons.' The shift was based largely on the realities that education and high level jobs are now available to women. China and India are making headway in this area after studying Korea's success, but their vast countries are more difficult to change quickly. But in Kino we followed quickly.

"Through equal opportunities in education and the job market, males are no longer preferred in the adult world so they are no longer preferred in the cradle."

--"As the father of a wonderful daughter I felt that the practice of aborting females, in China and other countries, was both sad and stupid. I would say the practice was "insane!" Heck, daughters are generally more concerned and loving. All sons do is play football, borrow and crash your car, then move away—showing their independence! In my experience women show both more practical intelligence and more actual intelligence. Their reasoning doesn't seem to be controlled by testosterone.

"Of course there is the reality that having more males in a population fits a society better for war. Killing off a million or so excess male youths has positive social ramifications for the sexually unbalanced society—and the war may result in the conquest of additional lands, so the rulers should feel more powerful. So if you are going to reduce excess males you will probably have to reduce wars! What an unthinkable idea!!"

--"As a woman I certainly agree. But in China they weren't involved in any major wars, so some societal problems developed as the excess male population reached adulthood. The heterosexual males had fewer chances to find mates so their opportunities to marry were certainly curtailed. With fewer men marrying there were far fewer babies. The population level plummeted even more than had been expected. The reduction of females in China has recently resulted in at least 40 million bachelors having no possibility of finding a Chinese woman for a mate. That's almost 15% of the 15 to 35 year old male population being left mate-less.

"Because of this, peasant women were tricked into coming to the cities with promises of good jobs, or they were kidnapped. The richer men paid the traffickers and married the prey. But that wasn't enough. Foreign women came voluntarily or were also kidnapped and helped to supply China's marital hunger. But foreigners have never been well accepted by the Chinese, with the exceptions of Marco Polo and Richard Nixon.

SEX IMBALANCE--GENDER EQUALITY

"As a result of the shortage of women, the classic 'seller's market' for females began to gain more status and even a bit of equality. The male to female birth ratios dropped from 160 males per 100 females in the early years of the 'one child policy' to 120 to 100. A normal ratio is about 105 to 100—because apparently the Y carrying sperm swim more quickly to the waiting ovum. But from the moment of conception on, the males out-die females at every age. China then decided that more women were needed so if the first child was a girl the parents were allowed to have another child.

"True gender equality has not yet arrived in China. You find it in some places, but most of the illiterates are women, most of the jobless are women. This has sparked some Chinese women to adopt the slogan of 'We cannot be fate's prisoners.'

"True equality, just as true freedom, comes when people are judged by their competence and their contributions to society, not the shape of their genitals or the color of their skin. To eliminate these ridiculous prejudices which are still found in China, we in Kino have enacted laws that allow for complete equality between the sexes. They were patterned after Scandinavian laws but are even more equalitarian in the way we enforce them. But it is more than just granting equal treatment to individuals. Even more important is the fact that more competent people are available to do the jobs that an efficient society needs, both in the workplace and in government. Our whole population has equal chances to succeed. Opportunities are no longer just for the male half of the society."

"Traditions, usually sanctified by religions, are the critical problem. Did you hear about the Ultra-Orthodox Jews in Israel attacking buses that carried ads encouraging women to pray at the Western Wall? Everyone should know that only men can pray at the Wall."

"So what else is new? The Koran says that women can be enslaved when their army has lost a battle. The Catholics won't let women into their church hierarchy. But fortunately the democratic ideal of freedom and equality are winning out in many places. Women as presidents, like me. Women as business leaders. Women as university presidents.

"I have to give the Scandinavian countries credit for much of this progress. It required quotas—but it got the job done. Your country helped with its affirmative action laws.

"I wonder if in your country job opportunities may even reverse because more females than males are opting for higher education."

--"I hope so. You mentioned equality of opportunity as the answer. But it is a major shift in tradition. I would think that overcoming the age-old traditions would be far more difficult than just opening up education and job opportunities."

--"As you well know, every historical shift, even the positive ones, bring with them some undesirable ramifications, such as prejudices, rebellions and worse.

"The Hebrew one God idea brought with it suspicions, wars and enslavements. Even today the ancient Jewish approach of over 3000 years arouses prejudice and even hate among many. When Jesus and Paul brought a newer form of monotheism, the Romans tortured them. Then when the Christians rose to power they tortured the unbelievers. Islam conquered North Africa, India, and Spain and forced major societal changes.

"When trains replaced horse drawn coaches, when planes replaced trains, and when autos replaced horses, society was forced to make huge adjustments to its traditions and in the way it worked. When mass production replaced hand work, society had to adjust.

"Ways of earning a living shift with the prevailing economic system. The number of workers required to supply the needs or wishes of the financially able consumers depends on the technological development of the producers, such as the efficient use of robotics or the hand produced goods of cheap labor.

"In medicine we have learned to look at the bio-medical model as the ultimate in health care. If something is wrong, a drug or surgery will fix it. But so often it is the environmental factors that are far more effective. Regular exercise, stopping smoking, controlling obesity, reducing fat intake are generally found to be far more important in living a longer life than taking many of the drugs that may reduce heart related problems. But if we have never exercised, have always smoked, have always eaten unhealthily, we generally prefer the solution that doesn't change our traditional life patterns. Better to pay a few hundred dollars a year for drugs and doctors and hope for good results than to cast aside our traditional unhealthy lifestyles.

"Every economic, social or political change requires adjustments. Many require adjustments to negative consequences. When the people's revolution replaced the Russian czar, Russian economics went backward. Through wars and pogroms, men disappeared. Women had more opportunities to advance through education. The overthrow of Communism brought some positive changes. But the Russian mafia emerged. The world moves by fits and starts. Some moves are little negatives, some are monstrous minuses. Some moves are small positives, some are mega-positives. We think that the one child policy has resulted in a huge economic plus with some relatively small temporary social setbacks. From the perspective of a 22nd century historian looking back at today's China and Kino, these countries and the changes they have enacted will be viewed as among of the greatest achievements of civilization—perhaps the greatest. And Kino is now leading the way for China.

SEX RATIO AND LICENSING

"Getting back to the discussion at hand, while amniocentesis was used in China to determine a baby's sex, in Kino we use amniocentesis for more than sex determination. We use it primarily to see if a potential child is free of hereditary disease and chromosomal problems. Our more recent advances have allowed the families to determine, through DNA analysis, the potential intelligence of the child. These techniques are not yet available in China. If parents definitely prefer a girl or a boy we in Kino can certainly determine the sex through amniocentesis.

"If the sexual ratio gets out of balance we give licenses only for the sex needed. If the conceived child is not the sex that was licensed, an abortion is performed, but the license is still valid. This doesn't happen often because our reproductive technology is such that we are over 90% certain that the proper sex will be conceived. We use centrifuges and other techniques to separate the X and Y carrying sperm and we use artificial insemination where necessary to insure that a pregnancy occurs. So it is not necessarily always left to chance. With the sex selection techniques you have pioneered in your own country we are now 100% certain in sex selection. Chinese officials are now seeing the merit in our approaches so I'm certain that changes will soon be evident.

"Maybe you can see the positive impact of the 'one child' policy. But in Kino we are trying to go even further than China in more positive ways by licensing parents by intelligent means."

-- "But with licensing, your population is getting older. Who will take care of the aged? How can you handle the retirement dilemma?"

--"Of course the average age of the population increases every year. But recognize that it's not only our problem, it is everybody's. From 2000 to around 2050 the median age of a citizen of the world will rise from 26 to 37 years. The graying population affects every economically advanced country. It is created by too low a retirement age and by significantly better medical care. From 1900 to 2000 the life expectancy in the U.S. rose from 48 to 77. That's almost a three years increase in life expectancy for every ten years.

"In 1900 a retirement age of 47 was possibly too old. Today a retirement age of 80 may be too young."

--"Certainly there's no question that the world is getting older. I guess we can't keep retiring at 50 or 60 or even 70. But I can't imagine any politician in the U.S. government telling people that they are going to have to work 5 or 10 years longer before they retire. There's no way they would be re-elected."

--"Commander, just look at the number of people over 65 in a population. From the beginning of this century to its halfway point, the over-60 population of the U.S. will rise from 16 to 26% of the population. In China it will rise from 10 to 32%. Japan, Italy, Germany and France have over 20% of their populations in that age range and they all have average ages of over 40. A few years ago we in Kino were even with Mexico with only 6 to 7% of our population that old. But our average age today is much older than Mexico's is today. The point is that we are all going to have the problem of a rapidly graying population.

"In the last 20 years, since 2000, modern day Japan's over-65 population has increased to about 25%—an increase of 40% during the last 20 years. Fewer children are being born since educated women are not marrying because the business world is more exciting than cleaning a house and cooking. And Japanese men don't pull their share of homemaking duties.

"So the problem is not just ours and China's, it's everybody's. Of course the size of the population of China makes it huge by global proportions, but comparatively speaking it isn't as bad as in many other countries.

"Because of the diminishing workforce most politicians, as well as many religious groups and trade unions, want to add more young workers so that the older people can still retire between 50 and 65. This is incredibly short sighted for the future of our finite Earth. More babies just add to the population and to global warming and to the lack of resources. Adding more people increases the world's problems far more than it diminishes them. But it may be good for politicians who won't face reality and for business people who are only looking at next year's bottom line. More young people will provide more consumers for the businessmen and more taxpayers to support old age pensions. And those young will soon be old, so even more babies will be needed. And we would be continuing the population proliferation and the explosion of toxic excesses and the disappearance of the essential resources of modern life.

"And if society plans to handle most of the pensions and refuses to make the workers responsible for themselves, there will always be a higher tax on the young to take care of the old if the population is stable, not growing. A growing population is easier to tax for retirees' pensions but the living conditions may not as good for retirees as their pensions are reduced—which is inevitable.

"We must face the realities. If the population keeps growing there would not be as much water for everybody. There will be more pollutions and more warming. There will be more problems relative to having sufficient electrical power or excess garbage. So there are plusses and minuses to a reducing population for those who decide to retire. While there may be some loss of income, there will be more of the basics to enjoy. Of course if the retirement age is increased there won't be a reduction of income.

"As people age, many want to retire. Some would like to have the option of retiring early. But at the same time many resent being forced to retire from jobs they love. The more interesting their jobs the longer people want to work, yet some countries, like Norway, force them into retirement. This is absurd.

"So the economic and psycho-social effects of the graying population can be minimized two ways. Those who want to work must be allowed to continue as long as they are capable of doing their jobs effectively. Second, workers must contribute enough to their retirement system so that they, not the government, have paid for their lifelong pensions. If they want to retire early or at a higher pension rate they must contribute more money to the pension system.

"China's pension plan for employees of state owned businesses allows retirement at 55. They assume 35 years of contributions from the workers then a retired lifespan of 15 years. We find that to be totally unrealistic. Thirty-five years of work then 15 years of retirement would require an annual contribution of over 30% of wages. This, of course, would be untenable for the worker. Then the life expectancy is actually 77 today, not 70 as was earlier assumed, and the life expectancy is rising every year. It seems that no government has been able to predict the future accurately. They always underestimate the problems.

KINO'S PENSION PLAN TODAY

"When Kino was given independence we immediately tackled the care of the elderly problem. We initiated a voluntary retirement program which was available once people reached 75. These people had paid nothing towards retirement during their working years so the state had to pick up the bill. We immediately set in motion retirement insurance payments for all workers. The optional retirement insurance and an optional retirement home placement insurance eliminated the need for male caretaking of the elderly.

"Originally it took a huge bite out of the national budget and required foreign borrowing. But as we now have both men and women in our highly technological workforce we have eliminated our national debt and good pensions and elder care are part of our income and 'value added' taxation load.

"We want to avoid the problems of the West. Here our workers pay a realistic amount into their retirement and health care accounts each month. They also pay for long term care. The payments never go into the state's coffers. The payments are invested by the state. If the investments pay what is expected there is always money for health care and when pension time comes the retirant can take an actuarially determined monthly income beginning at age 65. This is normally about half of the monthly salary. By age 70 it is about 65% of the monthly salary. By 80 it is 100%. Our life expectancies are 85 years at birth, due to our splendid health care system and the opportunity to exercise throughout our lives in our swimming pools, on our playgrounds, or on our bike paths. At the retirement age of 80 we expect another 12 years of life. As you know, life expectancy increases for every year we live. The percentages of expected retirement income, the age of retirement, and the changes in life expectancies change as the average age of the population changes.

"The state guarantees the payment, but so far has not had to contribute because the investment of the contributions has made more money than is needed. If a person dies, the total contributions are returned to his or her family, with 10% compounded interest. So you see it is a multifunctional savings account with a high rate of return.

"This next year we are moving to a more equitable plan. We have been working out the details for five years. Actuaries make their educated guesses about how long a person will live. We don't take the equalitarian approach that you do in America where women contribute as much as men and retire at the same ages and at the same pension rates as men. The facts are that generally: women live longer than men, small people live longer than big people, exercisers live longer than non-exercisers, married people live longer than single people, non-smokers live longer than smokers, the more highly educated live longer than the less educated, people with lower blood pressure live longer than those with high blood pressure, normally weighted people live longer than obese people, people whose ancestors lived longer tend to live longer than those whose ancestors died young, and so on. There are a number of such factors that are updated annually. All of these go into our data base. Every person submits an annual status report with the help of a doctor. Noted in the report will be such things as whether the person's weight changed positively or negatively, whether they began or stopped an effective exercise program, whether they stopped or started smoking, and so forth.

"Based on the individual's report and the changes in the risk factors in our society, everybody gets a longevity calculation every year. Based on these actuarially guessed factors a person can get an educated estimate on how long he or she will live. They then determine how long they want to work and at what salary they would need in retirement and adjust their pension contributions up or down.

"As with our previous plan, if a person dies before retiring his or her heirs get all the money put in with 10% compounded interest. If the retirant dies before using all the contributed money the remaining money, without interest is returned to the heirs. The money that the state has earned on the retirement contributions, which we hope is at least 10%, goes to pay those who outlive their contributions—so there is a government guarantee of a pension. After all, if our actuaries didn't figure it right, we are to blame.

"Because the working conditions are ideal and the job challenges are immense most Kinoese continue to work long past their retirement age. Many will take extended vacations or sabbaticals but eagerly return to their work on their return. We believe our system makes sense both economically and psychologically. Economically because every worker pays for himself through his contributions. Psychologically it allows people to continue to work full or part time if they desire. We allow four to six month sabbaticals every ten years throughout the working life to increase one's job skills or to study or travel to increase one's life satisfactions.

"In Europe today a person must work to about age 73 to take out about what he or she has put into the pension system. Yet most countries allow, or even require, retirement by somewhere between 55 and 67. Allowing retirements before age 73 requires that someone other than the retiree pay the pension. And with early retirements allowed, or even required, somebody else must pay for the retiree. It sounds desirable to allow early retirement. It certainly brings the politicians votes. But it makes no economic sense at all.

"Declining births reduces the number of workers per over-60 retiree. There were five workers per retiree 15 years ago, there will only be 2 in thirty years, at the century's halfway mark. Some countries plan is to raise retirement age by five years and to allow more immigration.

HANDLING TOO MANY NON-WORKING ELDERLY

"If too many old people are a big problem we could just kill them off when they are no longer productive, or at some agreed upon age. Of course we Asians wouldn't do this because we have great respect for older people. Your Native Americans are with us, probably because they came from here thousands of years ago. But you European-Americans seem to have such a self-centered way of looking at things and such a fetish for youth that you just tuck your old people away in rest homes strapped to their wheel chairs or sedated in bed, just waiting to die. And death is a blessing for all concerned. They are no longer draining the state's funds for elder-care, Medicare and Social Security. If they have money the state gets its cut and the children get theirs. No more need for the rest home visits that some consciences require. And still you fight euthanasia when an old person wants to die! Who wouldn't want to die when they are pained by illness and have no more social worth?

"Here in Kino our elderly are valued. We admire and heed their life experiences. We revere their link to our ancestors. We find that this continuity with the families of our past give us roots. But cultural and scientific change gives us branches. Together they let us grow to new heights."

--"It's a shame but I think your observations are too often true. And elder care costs are increasing as our population ages. There were 35 million people over 65 in my country when I left. It is now 55 million and in another twenty years it will be 85 million. The number of over-85s is increasing even faster. It was 3 million when I left, 7 million today and in another twenty years it will be 15 million. When I left it cost us $123 billion a year, today it is $207 billion, and in twenty years it will be $346 billion. Families often cannot take care of their elderly parents—or refuse to do so, and some elderly never had children. Maybe that's why they lived so long!

"We can't see the end of welfare spending—pensions, health care, eldercare. Do we tax more, borrow more, or just let everyone shift for themselves?

U.S. SOCIAL SECURITY

--"In Kino we don't expect that our young workers will have to support our retirees. It's not like your country where the Social Security payments largely go into the general budget and retirement payments come out of that budget. Too many retirees will eventually put an unmanageable strain on your younger workers."

--"That's true. The trust fund for my country's Social Security retirement system should be used up in 20 years, in 2040. The trust fund for Medicare, the health system for retired workers, has already been used up, in part because of the increased health costs and in part because workers' contributions are not enough to support the system. We now need several thousand dollars per taxpayer to pay for the complete Medicare package for the older part of our population.

"About 80 million baby boomers, those children born from the mid-40s to the mid-60s, were not effectively factored into the costs of caring for them in their old age. For this reason Ronald Reagan, rather than rely on tax increases on future generations, significantly increased the payroll tax rate with the idea that boomers would pay extra during their working years to build up a surplus in the Social Security Trust Fund. The extra money could be drawn upon when the boomers retired so it would maintain Social Security payments at designated levels. It took awhile, but by the time Clinton left office the federal government was actually running a large enough budget surplus that the Social Security System was working as designed.

"When President Bush took office in 2001 there was a projected budget surplus of $5.6 trillion over the next ten years. This would have gone a long way in paying off the $6 trillion national debt. Even before Bush took office the government had predicted that by now the national debt would start to skyrocket and in fifty years would be almost 200% of our gross domestic product. But because Bush increased, rather than decreased, the national debt we started our debt from a much higher level. It was eleven trillion dollars when he left office. We are now among the most indebted countries in the world and are having to forego our interest payments to our lenders, particularly China and Japan. Medicare and Social Security have had to be pared.

"Today the interest payments on the national debt equal the outlay for Social Security. Congress has had to keep increasing the national debt limit by trillions of dollars or the United States would have had to default on its debt obligations. Reducing taxes during the Bush years sounded good to the voters but every reduced dollar of federal income had to be supplanted by borrowing a dollar from somebody. Then there was the interest on the borrowing.

"As the baby boomers began retiring and utilizing Medicare fifteen years ago it increased the borrowing that our nearly bankrupt government had to do. But the legislators don't want to face the inevitable because it will cost their electorate money—and cost them votes. And you certainly don't want to do that! I think it's obvious that responsible governments cannot continue to spend more than they take in. Add to this that along with people retiring earlier and living longer our health care for the elderly is getting so incredibly expensive."

--"But commander, almost all countries owe some debt. And economists tend to agree that some debt is actually healthy."

--"That's true, but there is a level that is definitely economically unhealthy and a higher level that is deadly. That level is fast approaching because of tax breaks that didn't stimulate the economy as we were told they would, then the wars for democracy, then the increasing 'entitlements' that everybody wanted—Medicare, Medicaid, food stamps, Social Security, and many lesser programs.

"When Social Security was started there were 42 workers for each retiree. When I left on my voyage it was about 3 1/2 to 1, now it is about 2 ½ to one. Tell me that young workers are going to be taxed 25 to 50% of their salaries to pay for their parents' meager pensions! Luckily we have a trust fund for Social Security. Unluckily the government keeps borrowing it to pay for wars to stop terrorism or to spread democracy, for social expenses to keep the electorate content, and for pork barrels to keep the politicians and their financial backers happy. When Al Gore ran for president he suggested an untouchable 'real' account for the Social Security money. The voters rejected his proposal. So the taxpayers merely have to make up the payments through increased taxes to pay for the contributions they had already paid, but that had been spent by their elected representatives. It's kind of like asking a child to replace the money that a parent stole from the child's piggy bank, to buy a case of beer. Not exactly fair or far sighted.

"Just three years ago the Social Security payments began to exceed the payroll taxes entering the fund. Today the Social Security payment to retirees is about $100 billion more than is taken in. And in fifteen years there will be no money left.

"In the early years of this century the government in my country was adding nearly five trillion dollars a year to the citizens' debts. I remember reading an article early in my voyage that showed that every American household owed over half a million dollars at that time for Medicare and retirement benefits for federal and state programs and the federal and state debts. That was several years before the first baby boomers reached 65. It included: Medicare cost of $263,000; Social Security costs of $133,000, the national debt $43,000; military retirement benefits $25,000; state and local debt $16,000; federal retirement benefits $14,000; state and local retirement benefits $13,000; and a few other minor entitlements. (8) I wonder if I can just put it on my credit card. As long as I don't have to pay it off right now and can just pay the annual interest of $25,000. I guess I should feel lucky that I pay only about 3% interest with the government's treasury bill rate. What if I had to pay the 18% credit card rate! That would cost me $150,000 a year just for interest on my share of the national expenses. But as that noted philosopher of optimism, Alfred E. Neuman, has stoically counseled, 'What, me worry?' But then worrying might be appropriate when you consider that the national debt is seven times more than all of the private debt, such as home mortgages, car and credit card debt. And as taxpayers we owe it all—both our private and our public debts. Makes me feel all warm inside to know that whatever my legislators spend, I am responsible for. It's not like having somebody run up a tab on the credit card they stole from me, because the credit card company will pay the charges. But with the government's spending I pay even if I didn't order the $200 toilet seats for Air Force One, a war in Afghanistan, a war on jihadists, or the $50,000 in-depth study of the mating call of the Jamaican fruit fly."

--"I understand that historians are now rating Bush as the worst of all your presidents and Reagan as among the best. But they were both in the same party. I assume that their principles would have been similar."

--"Not really, Democrats are not all cut from the same cloth and Republicans are not all made from the same dough. It's about the principles of the leader. Is the leader honestly concerned with the good of the whole society, as you have practiced in Kino, or is the leader primarily concerned with a special interest group like the wealthy, particularly certain business interests such as oil or pharmaceuticals. Or is he more concerned with flaunting his power. Bush exemplified all of these negative motivations.

"But let's talk about your country. So many of your programs are very well thought out. How do your politicians work so effectively?"

--"Well we really don't have your type of politicians. We have single six year terms for the elected people—they are therefore not concerned with re-election. The people are elected to the legislature from several major employment groups: education, industry, health services, human services and several at-large members. The elections take place every 2 years so we always have two-thirds of the legislators with some experience. We have a total of 20 legislators. These people work with the career bureaucrats who advise the legislators and administer the programs. We don't have a judicial branch as you do so we can't have one judge or nine judges changing our legislature's laws.

"When agreement cannot be worked out we present the facts to the population on the evening news. We give all the positives and negatives as we know them. We don't use false statistics or shades of truth, or even lies, like we often see in the West. The populace, after hearing the pros and cons, register their preferences on a phone line connected to their television set. They don't just vote 'yes' or 'no', they can submit new ideas or they can indicate problems or advantages of the proposal. So we have a modified republic with the possibility or a true democratic input.

"This direct appeal to the electorate has aided us in not having the French or American style of special interest protests, such as the French students' job law protests or the American immigration protests. We want our people informed. What positive proposals might the students and unions have made that would also be accepted by the employers? After all, if the employers couldn't make it work they would just shut down or take their businesses to another country. And regarding the immigration demands, what would be the eventual advantages or disadvantages to the increased immigration of blue collar workers? In the West your protesters just seem to protest, without offering alternative plans. If our people are going to protest against something they must have an alternative.

"There is a tradition in China which is even more strongly adhered to in Kino, that is 'Honor the honorable.' Our tradition, not our laws, tend to govern us in electing representatives and in passing laws which should honor and enhance our society. Then our representatives are paid the same as their last job, so there is no financial incentive to govern. We again agree with Aristotle that we must not exhaust the public revenues by giving pay for the performance of public duties. Of course as he also said 'the smaller the population the more manageable it is.' And Kino is much smaller than your country."

--"In my country we have some very honorable men who have served as leaders and legislators, but we have also had people of less than admirable character. Along with their taking lobbyists' money to vote for special interests and bribing others by withholding a vote unless they include money for special 'pork barrel' interests, they hold stocks in companies they vote for even if it is not in the interest of the country. Then there are the trips and bribes given by special interest people that occasionally result in corruption charges. But these are rare because they protect their own. It is easy to see how the country got into the mess it is in economically. I sometimes wonder who is the greatest enemy, al-Queda or Congress and the President. Certainly our leaders have cost America much more in dollars than have bin-Laden and the other terrorists.

"There are some ethical positives. Some federal prosecutors are putting high level businessmen in prison for many years. Tyco, Enron and WorldCom are prime examples. If white collar crime is to be pursued as aggressively as organized crime and street criminals, there's hope for the country. But people in government seem to protect each other since so many hands seem dirtied. It is definitely difficult to find somebody who has not sinned and who will cast the first stone. But there do seem to be some calls by the voters to get values back in government. But the way pollsters and vote manipulating advisors seem to psychologically lead the voting herd, I wonder if real reform will ever be possible in my country.

The bad guys hammer down the good guys with their lies, misinformation and innuendos. It's a sad fact that the public usually buys it. Effective psychological techniques, rather than truth or reason manipulate our electors. Aristotle was right when he said, 'the masses will always remain impervious to reason.' Spinoza affirmed that observation writing that 'the people will always be ruled by imagination and emotion, not by reason.'

"But maybe your country is an exception to the pitfalls of democracy. You seem to be making progress far beyond what might be expected."

MAJOR CHANGES REQUIRE MAJOR ADJUSTMENTS—OFTEN TEMPORARY

--"We don't have all the answers but we are working on solving our problems. But let's recognize that without the one child policy there could not have been the rapid expansion of our economy. And of course those unborn will not have any babies, so it helped significantly to hoist China's economic anchor. It helped to unchain the financial miracle of the last fifty years and resulted in a major shift in the political status of China. And we in Kino are even ahead of the population reduction goals set by the Chinese. We are already in a population decline while we improve on the quality of our citizens by coming as close as we know how to giving every baby born in our country the best chance at being both loved and being successful.

"As we adjust to a smaller population, just like every similar country we are going to have to go through a few generations of strain. It will be more difficult for the young to find jobs. After a couple of generations the age groups within a population will stabilize and the young graduates will replace the older retirees.

"Major changes in a society such as China's are going to have major repercussions, but they will probably be less than those faced in the West and in Japan. As China's population ages, more families must support elderly members. In 1990 less than 4% of the population supported an aging person, by 2050 almost 50% will be doing it. This is just a momentary adjustment in human history. But from the historical perspective of the next century, it will be well worth it.

"But it is our tradition to not only care for our parents but also to honor them. As Confucius wrote 'Today when people call a man filial they mean that he is supporting his parents. But he does as much for his dogs and horses. If he does not show respect for his parents how is he differentiating between them and his animals.'(9) After all, our parents are our most immediate and important link to our ancestors. And our ancestors are revered, as is our glorious history.

"We in Kino haven't had the financial problems of elder-care to any great degree because China and some Middle East countries have been financially supportive—China because we are its appointed prodigy and the oil producers because we are an increasingly important market.

"But we, along with all countries that experience reduced population will have the problem of uneven employment for two generations or so. But this inconvenience pales when contrasted with the results of an increasing, or even a stable, world population. In the future, progressive societies will have to follow our lead. Mandatory retirements will have to be eliminated. Retirement ages will have to be raised. Just as births have to be reduced. And as medical science keeps us living longer, the adjustments will have to be 'adjusted' continually."

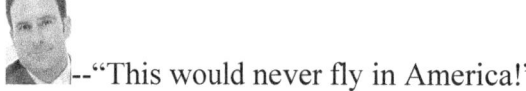--"This would never fly in America!"

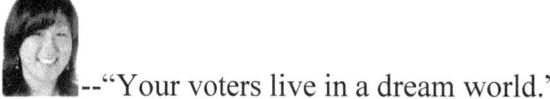--"Your voters live in a dream world."

--"They were raised on cartoons and Disney. They expect happy endings."

--"Prince Charming and the fairy godmother don't always save you at the end. The pot at the end of the rainbow is not always full of gold. Reality must sink in. In the front lines of a war the soldiers experience something very different from what they experienced in their computer games.

"This is the real world! People live longer. People will work longer. The French may riot for earlier retirement. But the government can't afford it. The English may strike for shorter work weeks. But those who want to eat will be working longer hours and longer weeks. The Japanese may expect lifelong job security from the firm they economically married. But if that firm is not productive in an area needed by the world—they are wedded to a corpse. The Americans may relax their immigration laws to let in hard working uneducated laborers. But these people will soon be replaced by robots. And the American budget will find that it will not be able to make the payments necessary for the illegal immigrants' medical and housing needs and the education of their children.

"There comes a time when we must become responsible for ourselves—keep our educations current for the changing needs of the global economy; save for our futures; take care of our own health; and if we want to retire someday, work long enough so that we have paid for it.

"We know that the future can't be intelligently planned without accounting for the road we have already traveled. We agree with your philosopher Friedrich Schiller that an historian is 'a prophet looking backwards'. We realize that we need not reinvent the wheel. We want to minimize making the mistakes of the past but we realize that the future of humankind has not been written by a god who has predestined us. We, as thinking people, have some measure of control.

"Perhaps we in Kino have been blessed by a looser more amorphous religious background. Most of us do not have the schizophrenic monotheistic God who is both vengeful and merciful, as do you in the West. We have a looser blend of the philosophical analysis of Lao Tzu with the yin and yang as competing, yet cooperating, aspects of our world. We have the secular sense of the relationships and order of Confucius and Mencius. We have our ancestral links extending back through the mists of our history and our prehistory. And we have the quiet simple ethical precepts of Siddhartha Gautama, the Buddha.

"Going back to Confucius and his cultural ancestors, there has been a deep feeling of respect and caring for our parents. It has always been the children, particularly the sons, who have had this responsibility. We now take a page from the Western concept of responsibility and see the state as also being responsible for the elderly. This seems more fair to the young and puts more responsibility on the individual for his or her own retirement years. But we want it sensibly administered. Each person should be responsible for himself as much as possible."

THE CHALLENGES

--"What have you seen as the challenges to your country as you have developed?"

-"We had to develop an educational system second to none. We needed to plan an economy that met the present and future needs of the world. For this we promoted both state planning and a free wheeling entrepreneurial business economy.

"Then we have our cradle to grave education. As your Henry Ford said 'Anyone who stops learning is old, whether at twenty or eighty. Anyone who keeps learning stays young. The greatest thing in life is to keep your mind young.' Learning is the most exciting thing we can do. We feel compassion for your people who must waste their hours playing poker or video games or glued to their televisions. It isn't that we don't understand that there are times for turning off the mind with passive recreational pursuits, but if our people have any recreational energy they use it to keep the body and mind moving forward. Most run or swim or cycle with their earphones delivering them the diamonds of literature, philosophy or classical music.

"One of our major industries deals with making education more enjoyable. We are diametrically opposed to that ancient idea that 'it doesn't matter what a person learns, as long as he doesn't like it.' Learning is fun and we keep looking for more enjoyable ways for our children and adults to learn. Cartoons, films, video productions, books, discussion groups, lectures, and many more avenues of adventure leading us to understanding ourselves and appreciating our universe.

"As you might expect, the higher living standards of Kino, the commitment to learning, the crime-free environment, and the potential to produce goods for the global economy, enticed productive people from the faltering economies of the West to immigrate. German engineers, American doctors and physicists, and British bankers were among those who were welcomed by the power elite of Kino. While the immigrants faced some ethnic discrimination because of their paler skins, they were accepted for their competencies. They were eager to lead a people hungry for success--after they had been punished through taxation for their competence and achievements in their own countries. But our laws forbad these immigrants from having children, except in exceptional cases. Mixing of races is not considered to be desirable by the government of Kino.

"A major scientific challenge was that we were pressured by China to develop cheap non-polluting power. Our government wanted to beat the goals set in Kyoto. But China was even more alarmed, as was Alpine Europe, when the glacier melting reached excessive levels. The glaciers on China's Qinghai-Tibet plateau were shrinking by 7% a year because the average temperature had increased by 2 degrees in the last few years. This would cause droughts, which could allow sandstorms. Sandstorms have become even more prevalent because forests have been chopped down.

"So our major environmental tasks have been to reduce the continuation of global warming and to reduce its effects, then simultaneously to solve the problem of a lack of fresh water—while reducing our population. Then, of course, we wanted to make certain that the children born in our country were assured of the most loving parents possible and had access to the best educational system in the world.

"When we look at our responsibilities, Kino is of course our primary concern. China is our second concern, then the rest of the world. Developing clean and cheap energy was obviously the major goal. It would eliminate the major sources of human caused global warming, it would allow us to use clean power to cool our homes and industries, and it would allow us to cheaply desalinate the ocean water. The extensive use of solar power really originated in our area, then Europe and the U.S. got into the act. Your state, California, really got things going when it offered billions of dollars of credits for the use of solar power. This gave all of us in the energy business a potential source of revenue.

"Ten years ago China tested a nuclear fusion device. They are also working on solar and wind energy and other sources of non-polluting or minimally polluting energy sources. They knew that using millions of gallons of oil and millions of tons of coal was a disservice to the world's environment. Just look at Denmark with more than 20% of its electricity produced by wind—more than 20 times the percentage produced in your country. And once oil passed $60 a barrel, wind became a financially competitive energy source.

"But from our founding we concentrated on studying solar power. We worked closely with the engineers at Shanghai University, which is in the forefront of solar research. We lured the highest level German solar engineers here with large amounts of Arab and Chinese cash. The Arabs have been interested because they want to continue leading the world as energy suppliers. That shouldn't be too difficult because they not only have more oil than most countries, they also have more sun! So when the oil and gas run out they will still be major energy suppliers if we can provide effective and inexpensive solar panels.

"Originally we ran parallel and cooperative research for producing cheaper energy and cheaper water. We experimented with silicon, orgasmic polymer, quantum dot and other more effective substances for power and in nanotechnology for developing efficient filters for the sea water. The power for the desalinization came from developing electrical power from the mechanical potential of the ocean waves near the desalinization plants and from power developed by the ebb and flow of the tides."

--"My father had always wondered why it had taken so long to develop effective solar power. He told me that in the 1950s he had a solar powered radio that he used to take to the beach when he was lifeguarding at Venice Beach."

--"As I understand it, it was a combination of factors, such as that other energy was so cheap and the modern materials for catching photons were not developed. But as the need for non-polluting energy became essential, huge amounts of research money came from governments and industry. Both private and public researchers then found it profitable.

"Our other major problem was to find a cheaper source of pure water. The UN estimated that 130 million people in China used contaminated water. Then with the glaciers melting, a major source of fresh water was being eliminated. China attempted to help its situation by building dams. This helped but didn't solve the problem. We have to desalinate a good part of our water, but we reuse waste water after it is purified. Farms and industry are able to use the re-purified water. Our homes have two water supplies, one for fresh water and another for the re-purified water for washing our bodies, our clothes and dishes and for our gardening.

"Our work in developing affordable energy, producing fresh water, and recycling waste water not only helped us and China but we had solutions and technologies that the world needed now. This is the real source of our wealth. Water production and conservation is nearly a trillion dollar business and we have a huge chunk of it. We have improved on a home appliance that pulls water vapor from the air. Every home and business will soon have one. They will each pull 75 gallons of water from the air every day.

"We use and re-use the water, from clean drinking water to waste water and industrial cooling water and finally to hydroponic agriculture, then the steam is often captured and used again in the same cycle. We have paid back those who loaned us money and now we are debt free. We can therefore put our own money into making a better life for our people. But we all know that people want to work in creative and productive jobs. We are not going to compromise the essential nature of a sound work ethic. So we put our money into better education, better libraries, better parks and pools, and better musical productions of opera, musical theater and symphonies. We want the accoutrements of life to be superb."

BENEFITS OF REDUCING POPULATION

--"You have certainly done a remarkable job. Yet with all of your accomplishments things are not hustling and bustling. I feel a real sense of peace here in Kino. And I do want to use your recreational facilities and experience your musical presentations. I think every culture has something to teach other cultures, or they wouldn't have endured. There are beautiful philosophies from both the East and the West. There are arts and music that are eternal arising from most cultures.

"On the other hand, the urge to war seems to be a cultural universal. Do you think that in the future the 100 year old leaders will be sending the 60 and 70 year olds off to war?"

--"Commander, you may have the urge of a military man, but I think the retirees would be too smart to go. I wonder if we will be smart enough to avoid big wars in the future. Or will we settle for a major gas attack that wipes out a country's population so that the attacker can just move in and take over the water, the housing and the factories? Or will the next war be my robots against your robots?"

"Hopefully as we reduce populations and increase the abilities of people to reach beyond their selfish natures and embrace the widened social concerns necessary for a caring modern society, we can reduce the overpowering need to conquer that has been the hallmark of what we have called civilization. From Alexander to Zengh, from Attila to Hitler, from Caesar to Genghis, we see selfishness collectivized and violence applauded until perhaps the final nuclear curtain may undo it all.

"Which lands conquered still remain with the conquerors' kin? None. But what are the legacies of the mental conquerors, Socrates and Aristotle, of the Christ, the Buddha, the Prophet—their legacies still stand and expand. It is clear that the results of mental struggles and conquests are far more lasting than those of the sword."

--"But haven't some of the followers of those saints also turned violent and sought to establish earthly kingdoms?"

--"All too true. The spiritual kingdoms of the great teachers have been blasphemed by those who don't understand them."

"From my Asian point of view it seems that the popes and ministers have misdirected the teachings of Jesus. The imams and muftis have subverted the teachings of Muhammad, and the Jews have left the beliefs of Abraham. Would Jesus be concerned about speaking in tongues? Would Muhammad bless the violence of the jihadists? Would Abraham agree with the violence of the Israelis? I think that Moses might. But these wars seldom happen in the mental world, the world of the intellect. Have you ever heard of a war to spread the teachings of Aristotle or Kant?"

--"OK, now the big question. Tell me about your population control ideas and how they work."

LICENSING IS A NECESSITY

--"The theory of population control has been refined through the years. From a "one child per family" policy enforced by societal pressures, then a law controlling the one child policy, and now the society of Kino requires a license to have a baby. In Kino we can handle the population we have, but that's not the point. We want to lead the world in intelligent population control. We need to further reduce our population for the good of the world.

"We see effective parenthood as critical for an efficient forward moving, peaceful society. We know that our children are the future of our society. But we don't see it as a biological right for people to have children. Our citizens are not hermits, we live together. We value both individual children and our society. It is just that we are no longer living in the agricultural world of a few millennia ago when we had only a few million people tramping around the planet.

"The ineffective expenditure of our limited resources on trying to repair children and adults who have been damaged by incompetent parenting makes setting standards for parenting necessary today. Setting minimum standards for parenting would help to prevent child neglect and abuse. We should not continue to wait until parents damage their children physically and emotionally. We need to weed out the potentially ineffective parents and educate those who can be good parents by giving them every help we can. Of course every young potential parent thinks it's easy to do everything right, while older parents wonder if they did anything right!

"Protecting society from inefficient parents is like cancer protection, it seems that only about 5% of cancer cells cause most of the problems. We think that more than 5%, perhaps around 10% of parents may not be acceptable either because of genes or because of poor parenting abilities or aptitudes.

"Licensing parents lays the foundation for dramatically reducing the need for costly and ineffective governmental welfare and correctional programs. It affirms parental responsibility for child-rearing and reduces the need for governmental involvement in defective families. It increases the general level of competent parenting and positively affects generations to come."

--"I can only imagine what my nation would be like if every child had competent parenting. This may not be an unrealistic goal if we really care about our future. Every ineffectively raised child becomes a potential burden on our future and a citizen who cannot make a maximal contribution to our society through economic or humanitarian performance. I would guess that you would agree with me that any rights of parenting must give the potential child the total right—any rights that adults might want because they want children should have no validity. Of course this flies in the face of all human tradition. Can intelligence or laws reverse the flood of our natural desires and expectations? I hope so. At least China and Kino have put their societal fingers in the dike of one of humankind's overwhelming historical forces."

"How do you handle the licensing here in Kino?"

--"Licensing is handled by the social service agencies. Any people denied licensing can appeal or they can follow the recommendations of the agency on how to remedy their inadequacies through education or other means. We are not trying to deny couples having children, only to make certain that they are financially and psychologically ready—and that their child will be an asset, not a detriment to the whole world. By subscribing to the one child law we are reducing our population. We hope that the world will follow our lead."

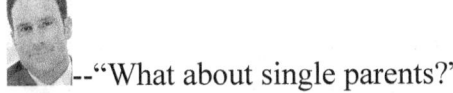--"What about single parents?"

--"They have to pass the same license requirements as couples. This, of course, may be twice as difficult. Their psychological abilities may be equally as great, but they may have problems meeting the time commitment required to raise young children. They may, however, be quite acceptable for adopting children who are at least three or four years old.

"As Confucius indicated, we needed a population that is intelligent and psychologically sound. This was the most difficult thing we have had to deal with in our young country. Talk about tradition! Our population had already lived with the 'one child' policy. That challenged a major societal tradition. But the people can now see for themselves the benefits of the reduced population for our society and for themselves. The tradition of having unlimited children was far more deeply ingrained in China than merely licensing, as we do in Kino. Our approach to licensing is merely determining when the pregnancy can occur. Then we are trying our best to insure that the parents are aware of what a child's needs are as it grows."

--"Haven't you had objections from people because their individual rights or religious beliefs are violated?"

RIGHTS

—"Not really. We don't have scriptures revealed to us by a monotheistic god. Perhaps we are thereby blessed! We don't have that single deity to pray to, to bless our activities whether warlike or peaceful, and to ascribe our fortune or misfortune to. We, as a people, have the power to do what we will. As a people, society has to be primary. While we recognize that some individual desires, which you often call 'rights', may sometimes be shunned, we realize that the forward thrust of the whole society must be our major concern. The totalitarian Communism of Mao certainly had many major faults. The needless deaths of millions and the failed economic experiments were certainly major negatives. But the totalitarian rule is responsible for the progress we have made the last forty years.

"What you call democratic ideas are now more often coming into play. Freedoms are more evident. But not every freedom is good for society. When a freedom allows for more diversity, it can get into the way of progress. Having more Muslims, Christians, Hindus and Falun Gongs gives more competing ideas as to how society can progress. On the other hand, allowing freedoms of entrepreneurs and freedom for better educations can help the society. The problem is that no one knows exactly the right mix. The Shi'ites think they know. The Sunnis think they know. The Lutherans think they know. The Amish think they know. The Catholics think they know. The atheists think they know. The Republicans think they know. The Democrats think they know. The Green parties think they know. The kings think they know. The revolutionaries think they know. Where is the truth? Isn't truth usually in the eye of the beholder? What is important as a progressive society is that we follow the successful paths and eliminate the unfruitful paths.

"Every time you eliminate an unfruitful path you step on some toes, you trample what some believe to be their 'human rights.' When we put in dams for water conservation and to develop non-polluting hydro-electric power we stepped on the toes of thousands of farmers. We lost many yuan in agricultural production but we gained much more in essential economic infrastructure, then we quickly made up the economic loss of rice production in high technology products. The country profited far more by building the dams. Such action required a strong central government and accurate farsighted planning. It didn't take a genius to see the need for the dam or to evaluate its worth compared to the pain suffered by those forced to leave the land. But it did require a strong central government to make it happen as fast as possible.

"The problem with a strong central government of a huge country is that positive ideas may not make it through the bureaucratic channels. That is why entrepreneurs have been encouraged. Could Bill Gates have started Microsoft in 1975 in China? No way! Could he have started it in Kino today? Yes, and probably easier than it was in the U.S. in 1975. We nurture excellent individuals and excellent ideas. We finance them. We market them. We are streamlined for the global economy.

"We are a society-based country with some individual rights. We don't allow structured religion. We keep our focus on what is best for society. We believe that religion is not compatible with the freedom to progress. People are always wondering if God approves. To develop a utopian society you can't be hobbled by the competing certainties of the several religions. Bishops and ayatollahs gain too much power and can strangle progress with their personal preferences, which their God always approves. I wonder, too, why each successive revelation seems to favor a different group with the unprovable insights to the Almighty's absolutes.

"Look at the problems religions cause China   Tibetan Buddhist monks and nuns are said to be imprisoned and tortured for acts of peaceful dissent. The rebellion against the rules in China have always had some roots in a religion. We want to avoid it in Kino.

"Human rights groups regularly try to force us to allow religion. We just deny them visas. So many of the 'human rights' people want everything for the individual even if it is bad for the society. In effect they are pushing for anarchy.

"If people do not like our society as it is being handled or as it changes, they are free to leave. And since they are well educated and can take their wealth with them, including their accumulated retirement benefits, they are welcomed most places. But few leave. Our traditions, dating back 4,000 years, lead us to expect a benevolent government. Belief in a supreme being, particularly a monotheistic God, has never been a part of our tradition.

"The young are expected to follow the elders. This was expressed well by Confucius, but the tradition had probably been in existence for centuries. Of course as our young become more familiar with what is going on in the West, they want instant 'freedoms'. We think that such freedoms are often not well thought out. For example the French students' violence in opposing a liberalized employment law because they didn't get everything they wanted, or the rallies of illegal immigrants in the U.S. for their 'rights' both seemed ill advised. The young will always be jealous of the mature citizens who have proven their worth. We must face up to the fact that the young are impulsive, and often uninformed. They seldom have the maturity or the factual backgrounds to make informed decisions.

"If we allowed religions to exist we would just add more arguments to attack our society's structure. Just look at the societally destructive approaches that religions can bring—Christians versus Christians, Muslims versus Muslims, Muslims versus Christians, Muslims versus Hindus, Christians and Muslims for or against Jews, Jews versus Jews. We don't need any of that. When you talk with Dr. Wang tomorrow I'm sure you can go into more depth relative to the possible conflicts and differences of opinion that religious values and society values often develop.

"Five hundred years ago the Chinese emperor allowed Christian missionaries. Then a later emperor stopped it and sent the missionaries packing. So there has been precedent for both the allowance and the disallowance of outside religions and for their control by the Chinese government. In China today they are allowing some religious beliefs. They did this under communism but it is more pronounced now. The present government wants a tight control on religion. For example those who want to follow the Catholic religion must be members of the Chinese Patriotic Catholic Association. This group has even appointed its own Catholic bishops. The Vatican vehemently disapproved. There have been Muslim groups in China for a thousand years. And of course Buddhism in some form has been around for two thousand years and in its Mahayana approach has combined with the tradition of the veneration of ancestors and the teachings of Confucius and Lao Tzu. This could be said to be the most common form of Chinese religion. They sort of accepted everything.

"The uneducated people need beliefs in an afterlife and of some supernatural powers who can be prayed to for impossible favors or blamed for catastrophes. Such deities or forces of nature seem to be found in every primitive group. And I would have to say that most of us on this earth are still primitive. We think we are advanced—but we know very little. Every age is convinced that it knows all and that its gods are real. But that, too, passes away. A more sophisticated god appears. A more powerful brand of prayer or meditation appears. A more broadly based humanitarian world view is proposed. But the people generally still believe in the gods of their parents and flaunt the ethics of the religions they ostensibly follow. We want to keep things down to earth without all the theological mumbo-jumbo.

"We have enough arguments among the society-centered people—communists, socialists, and free enterprisers. We have arguments about globalization, whether it is good and if so how much is good. We have arguments about which individual desires should become rights. Should we allow psychoactive drugs, if so which ones? When youth attempt to show their power in clubs or gangs, what sort of activity should be allowed. What about prison sentences? Should they be long or short, should we keep the death penalty, should prison be used to punish or rehabilitate? How much income should be taxed, and from what sources—income, sales taxes, luxury taxes, property taxes? You see we have enough problems to solve.

"There is always a problem when you step on toes that haven't been stepped on! People don't complain about having to take drivers' tests or driving at the speed limit because those restrictions developed as the automobile developed. But tell people that they should not eat red meat or potatoes and they keep on doing it. Of course those are merely traditions, not laws. But when you require or forbid something that has never been required or forbad before, and make it under the force of law, you get resistance—often major resistance. If the county gets permission to cut down a tree, given its environmental importance, someone may chain themselves to that tree. If houses are condemned to put in a needed highway, somebody will inevitably refuse to leave, no matter how much they are paid for the house. Only the law, enforced by the police, can solve the problem for society. Not many things attack our emotional beings like when our reproductive desires are quelled or our attachments to our dwellings are disrupted. We don't really have problems with either. The one child law has been accepted. Additionally many married couples do not want children. They find more joy and fulfillment in their jobs and in each other's companionship. They have much more freedom. Of course you have found this in the West already. Southern Europe and the upper middle classes in your country have shown real reticence to having children. Then there are so many who choose not to marry so that they can dedicate themselves to their professions.

"Certainly in Kino we have the problem of self-centered interests versus the interests of society. Just as when someone is denied a license to drive a car or a license to practice medicine, the individual is saddened but the society is better off. Rights in a society come from the government of that society. They don't come from individual desires. When Patrick Henry said 'Give me liberty or give me death.' He was expressing his own selfish interests while working for a society that would indulge his passion.

"We have freedom of political speech. People can say what they want regarding policies of government or economics. But they don't have the right to every type of free expression. They don't have the right to produce or view pornography because it debases some humans, usually women and children. They don't have the right to criticize police or women in their songs, but they can complain about the police in legitimate protest in the newspapers or in government hearings. There is no freedom to put down other religions or races. So even though we don't allow your one-God religions we will not allow them to be belittled. We have strong laws against psychoactive drugs. We allow some alcohol use but if a person becomes drunk he loses his license to buy alcohol for a year. Our educational system is quite strong on teaching the problems of using alcohol and other drugs. But it is the society's intolerance for altering one's highest mental faculties that is the major inhibitor of using drugs.

"While the people of the Netherlands are given the rights to marijuana use, prostitution and euthanasia, people in the United States are not always given these rights. If some Americans want these rights they need to move to the Netherlands or fight for changes in the laws so that their desires will become their 'rights'. They did this in Colorado regarding marijuana use. They did it in Oregon for euthanasia.

"While China has a death penalty that is easily declared, our death penalty laws give many protections to the adjudged. But unlike your country, death penalty inmates are not given their freedoms on legal technicalities. If they are guilty they are quickly punished. Also, they don't have unlimited legal appeals. But the evidence against them must be substantial.

"The message of Karl Marx was that we must prepare for the future. Your Western politics seem to be concerned with the immediate. Vote in people who will lower the gas price today, who will reduce taxes today, who will build more roads today. Your leaders follow the crowds. They develop their policies based on the latest polls. The world needs vision. Jefferson had it. Lincoln had it. Wilson had it. But most of the recent visions in your country often come from outside of your government.

"Martin Luther King had a vision of racial and religious freedom. Bill Gates had a vision of worldwide communication and has a vision of how to wipe out poverty and disease. Today's globalized world needs leaders who can help us head off the environmental and economic Armageddon that will engulf us if we deal only pragmatically with the present. Changing our inevitable future will not be smooth. There will be bloodied noses and broken arms that will hurt today but will not even be noted by the inhabitants of the future—if a future will be. It's like the proverbial ostrich, if we keep our heads in the sand long enough someone will steal our feathers for a hat, then someone will take our skin for shoes, then someone will take what remains and serve it as a gourmet treat."

--"You make a good point. We had better take our heads out of the sand –soon, like today! That brings me to the question of your educational goals and your education system."

EDUCATION

--"As the world has become more scientifically modern the essential nature of the educational system of each country comes more into focus. While nearly every politician promises a better education for the citizens, in reality the education budget is often the first item to be slashed. Because teachers are not adequately paid, fewer potential teachers are educated. And while the truly dedicated teachers might teach for half of what they earn, far more potential teachers are turned away by the lack of respect for the profession and the lack of salary to pay for a comfortable life.

"In Kino we have put educational funding on the front burner—and it has paid off. International tests show that the Kinoese students do as well or better than other Asian students. And certainly Asian students have usually come out on the top of the international rankings. Where Kino has excelled is that while requiring our students to learn the essentials by rote, as European and Asian students have traditionally been taught, we have also worked to develop a creative learning environment which has been more the tradition in the more effective schools in the United States. So the Kinoese have developed the memorization skills necessary for basic thinking and they have concurrently developed the problem solving and creative skills necessary for advancing in our modern world. The educational systems of Kino have far surpassed those of the U.S. as the

Americans have begun judging their schools on how they perform on objective rote memory tests while they have had to reduce the creativity emphasis.

"In science things must be measurable. How can creativity be measured on objective tests? How can creativity be taught while preparing for standardized tests that measure knowledge accumulated? The young Einstein and Edison would again fail their tests if they were to be tested in America.

"The Chinese universities award four times the number of advanced degrees annually as the US and they are tough. But it is difficult for college graduates to find jobs. Some come to us. We have our own universities and they are top notch. Our level of universities is slightly higher than in the U.S. The Harvards, the Berkeleys, the UCLAs, the Stanfords are equivalent to our schools, but we don't have the low level or the mail order doctorates that have been increasingly finding their way into American academia."

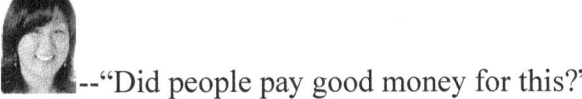--"Yes I know what you mean. In California anyone could set up their own university and give bachelor, master or doctor's degrees. You merely had to put up a bond of $10,000 which costs a thousand dollars a year. You didn't need any academic qualifications. Then because the university was set up under California law the state recognized the degrees for many state licenses. There used to be a number of state licensed psychologists who had such non-accredited doctoral degrees but had no competence. I don't know if this ridiculous opportunity still exists. I'll have to check it out.

"I knew a woman who was so proud of her 3 college units for a 3 page paper on how she taught roller skating. When I heard that, I went to her 'university' to look at the doctoral dissertations there. The 'university' was in a 3 room house on Wilshire Boulevard. I didn't find a single footnote in any doctoral thesis. I asked the 'president' of this university about it. I thought it was strange because my masters' thesis had over 200 bibliographical citations in my second chapter. He said that he wanted the student's knowledge to unfold from within and not be cluttered by the research of experts."

--"Did people pay good money for this?"

-- "Yes and no. Because California had certified the universities the students were entitled to federal education loans. So money that was supposed to go to legitimate students in legitimate universities found its way into unworthy pockets. These so-called schools had no hope of ever getting a legitimate accreditation so they started their own accrediting agency for non-traditional schools. It made them look legitimate in their magazine, internet and newspaper ads."

-- "Are those the advertisements I see in international papers for these illegitimate schools?"

--"Some are, but some are for borderline but accredited schools, and some are for high level universities.

"Most legitimate academic universities are now aware of these diploma mills so when people apply for jobs they require official transcripts of the grades. But I've seen people work into the professorial level of foreign universities with phony degrees. I had a friend who was evaluating a Scandinavian for a position in a legitimate university. He had one of these faked degrees. And he was already teaching at a Norwegian university. In Scandinavia they are usually so honest that they can't conceive of someone producing a worthless degree and passing it off as legitimate. But let's get back to the education in Kino. I've noticed that there are so many Orientals playing in the world's symphony orchestras, and they seem to be particularly often heard as soloists."

THE ARTS

-- "That's true. In Asian countries 8 of 10 children learn to play a musical instrument. It is no surprise that Asians are leading the world in classical music performance. Here classical music is appreciated by the young as well as the old. In America few young people stray from their rock and hip-hop long enough to appreciate real music."

--"Certainly learning to play an instrument is a time consuming recreation. I don't think it has the lucrative potential of playing quarterback, striker or power forward, though."

--"I know that Americans, when given the choice, will work more to amass more money. Europeans will opt for the time to relax. In Kino we're caught in between. Our traditional

60

poverty and our peasant-inspired seven day workweeks have inspired us to work hard when we see some potential for our financial futures. We want more if we can get it. It's like the bear overfeeding before hibernation. But we don't hibernate. At the same time we have a reverence for beauty. We want to create and enjoy the arts of the eye, the ear and the palate."

--"In just the few hours I've been here I have certainly experienced the ecstasy of your aesthetic soul. The dinner was an incomparable joy to my palate, tastes that exceeded my mind's culinary dreams. The architecture is magnificent. Only in Spain have I sensed the elegance of imagination to rival it. And the heavenly sounds of your ancient qin and pipa airing Eastern and Western classics, then the violinist playing Tchaikovsky's violin concerto—my favorite. You seem to have eagerly joined the best of the Eastern and Western worlds."

--"You have the saying that people 'do not live by bread alone.' We certainly believe this. We give all students the opportunity to appreciate their bodies in a comprehensive physical education program. We give them the opportunity to understand history and philosophy. We pursue the great literature and the arts from both the East and the West. This is along with their rigid mathematics and science curriculum. We have taken a page from your American high schools and colleges relative to extra-curricular activities. So we have music groups, both orchestras and vocal groups. We have speech and debate teams, language clubs and other recreational groups. We also have sport teams, dance and play production activities.

"We encourage cradle to grave education and recreation. Our colleges are open day and night. Our people can pursue, without cost, higher education or recreational opportunities. As opposed to most countries, we pay our teachers very well, so well that we have huge numbers of foreigners applying for the jobs. Our teachers are retained only if they are exceptional. They must have a great deal to offer academically and they must excite the students with their style and substance.

"We have taken a very different tack in our university hiring than you have in the West. Over the years your university hiring has become open to only people with doctorates who have published extensively in academic journals that very few people read. Those who have studied in your universities often observe that quite often the great researcher is a poor teacher. Some can teach their single area of expertise well, but traditionally college professors are asked to teach several quite different courses.

"When we want research done it is done in our research facilities. Sometimes these researchers will teach a class or two in their area of expertise. But that is up to them. And if their evaluations are not high in the classroom, they will be terminated from their supplementary teaching duties.

"We think your emphasis on research that is often meaningless is often cheating your students. Your universities have become so research oriented that teaching has become superfluous. We do have some research facilities in our universities but in most cases they are separated from the teaching facilities. We have some crossover, we do have some teachers who do research and some researchers who teach. Their pay can come partly from the research institute and partly from the teaching institute. At the master's and doctoral levels there is usually a crossover with students taking classes but also working with researchers.

"We concentrate our research in the areas of global warming and desalinization. We also do some research on weapons, particularly lasers and satellites. We let the British, Germans and Americans study ancient Egypt, organ transplants, and Tibetan literature. We merely read their work. Our work, at this stage of our development is in those hard sciences that may make life on earth more of a possibility. And of course we have to have defensive weapons.

"We realize that not everyone will be happy with our national goals. They are free to leave. We have one who is fascinated with ancient Egypt. She is now with the Egyptian Department of Antiquities. I am fascinated with the times of the pharaohs. All students study it as apart of their ancient history course in high school. But if they want to study more they must go abroad. We have one of our graduates teaching Twentieth Century American Literature at the University of Washington. One teaches sport sociology at Penn State. One teaches early Chinese history at Beijing University. We know that no society can offer everything to everybody. Our citizens are always free to leave if they can find a country that will take them."

VALUES

--"But from what I have seen and what you have told me, you want to experience the broad range of human thinking and achievement."

-- "But we cannot progress towards understanding our highest selves and the development of a realistic utopia unless we effectively combine the knowledge of modern science, the conveniences allowed by technology, and the aesthetic broadening of the arts all tied together by a comprehensive theory of values that allow for individual achievement and enjoyment in an ever-advancing society.

"We recognize that life is a series of choices, societal, religious and personal. Our lives will be better or worse based on the choices we make. Choose to smoke or not, to vote or not, to work hard or not, to further our education or not. Our lives and our societies are dependent on the types of choices we make and whether we follow them through.

"While we value freedom of thought, we want to develop a national psyche that is society based. We want to reward education and human enterprise but emboss them in a fabric of social responsibility.

"We want our values based as much as possible on facts. Facts are not influenced by emotion or prejudices."

--"But don't your societal values often conflict with people's self centered interests? We all want solutions to our problems but we generally want somebody else to solve them. We need to recycle. Let somebody else do it. We need to drive our cars less. Let somebody else take the bus. We need fewer babies. Let other people limit their families.

"It is a problem of values. For example, there are some people who believe that humans are responsible for solving their problems and others who believe that God will provide. This brings up such questions as whether we must limit population for the good of society or increase population because God said to 'be fruitful and multiply'. I wonder if we need to have more souls born so that they can be saved so they can find their way to heaven.

"Early this century in the US elections, the Christian right voted in Republicans so that 'moral values' could be followed in the country. Their values were unclear. What did the Bible have to say about abortion, cloning, prayer in schools, stem cell research, or countries being governed by religious values? Didn't Jesus say 'to render to Caesar that which is Caesar's and to God the things that are God's'. Did he advocate a separation of church and state? It seems so!

"Did those religious values include the government spying on its electorate. Did those values encompass illegal lobbying, money laundering, obstruction of justice, child molestation, adultery and all of the other illegal actions done by the high ranking members of the party advocating religious and family values. While these illegal behaviors are not atypical in human history, it pains me to see lawmakers, public administrators and judges who so loudly proclaim their religious values but trash them in their daily lives. Since college I've been a Republican. I was proud to be a Reagan Republican. He seemed to live his values. But since that time I have seen only few bright beacons leading me. Rather I trail Diogenes with his lantern—looking for an honest man. Or maybe I should say, looking for an honest leader.

LICENSING REQUIREMENTS

"That brings me to your area of social policy that intrigues me the most—licensing parents. Obviously parents should begin to make the decisions that will affect their child well before pregnancy occurs. Parents should know what it will cost and what will be expected of them. Once two people have decided to become parents and the mother is in good health, the decisions will begin to snowball from the moment of conception. It is the parents who are largely, if not totally, responsible for the way their children turn out. Did they become statesmen or thieves, inventors or tyrants, artists or killers? Parents are, indeed, the creators of destiny. What does your licensing theory do to increase the probability of ensuring effective parents?"

--"Ten years ago I signed into law a bill for the compulsory licensing of parents in our country. The concept was born years ago, but it was repugnant to us then. We had seen laws in Europe which forced the sterilization of certain unfit people so that their societies would be improved. We had observed the laws in many of your states which allowed for compulsory sterilization. But most of all, we had noted the unprecedented increase of inmates in jails and mental institutions around the world. This great increase of criminals, terrorists and other people who are mentally ill brought it forcefully to our attention that many people were not qualified for parenthood. So we took the logical next step in population control.

"Our law required that people who wanted to have children demonstrate that they were economically capable of raising a child. We all know that, for too many years, the state had to support too many children. The law also required that people desiring to have children demonstrate a knowledge of the decisions necessary for effective parenthood. They would have to pass examinations concerning nutrition, diseases, emotional health, and mental development. They also had to submit some evidence of their own emotional stability and their genuine desire to have children.

"All loving parents want to give their children whatever physical and emotional ingredients are necessary to make that child the best that it can be. Unloving parents, those who want children for the wrong reasons, are the ones we are attempting to eliminate. They are the ones who want children for themselves rather than for the sake of the child.

"In the 18 or so years that the child is under the parents' custody the parents will be determining the physical, intellectual and emotional structure of the child. Many thousands of inputs will determine the body and character of the future adult. But where can the parent look for guidance? The myriad of books often confuse the baffled parent even more. We want to give them the best information that the sciences have to offer on child raising. Your President Kennedy said truly that "Children are the world's most valuable resource and its best hope for the future." It is the children, not the parents, who are our major concern—for their own sakes and for the sake of the society.

"The idea that having a baby is a natural right of any person regardless of their age, mental health, or knowledge of parenting, is an idea whose time has finally come to an end. We now realize that the decision to have children is at least as important as being able to drive an automobile or operate a citizens' band radio, both of which have required licenses for years. It was the belief of our legislature and myself that this law will benefit society in general--but particularly the parents who should not have had children, and the children who will now be born with more capable parents. We further believe that each child born in this country should have, as a birthright, parents who honestly want the child and are prepared to care for that child.

"The license requirements included: that the parents be at least 25 years old and have a stable relationship. Additionally a pre-license agreement on child support should the relationship break up; and a one year course on parenting for prospective parents were required. The parental education course is required one night a week for three hours. This course covers understanding how to love; the necessity and the types of discipline; the costs of a child; and the nutritional, physical, and health needs of a child from conception to adulthood.

"A person can opt out of that class by passing an extensive test on the content of the class. During this one year course they are required to spend 30 hours in a home for the aging, 30 hours in a pre-school and 16 hours in a maternity ward. The objective here is to let them judge whether or not they are capable of loving. They must determine whether they have the psychological ability to be caring and to help a child or an elderly person to achieve their needs. After these experiences we find that some volunteer more time, some decide to change their occupations to these care-giving vocations, and some find that their selfish desires are greater than they thought and opt out of the licensing process. Some even divorce because their desires for children have diverged so much.

"We also teach about sex and sexuality. It is appalling how few people understand the basics of conception, pregnancy and birth. We would like them to know how babies are born in Kino. For example, in France, girl babies are found in roses, and boy babies are found in cabbages.

In the United States, storks bring the babies. In all other countries, babies are born naturally, requiring the reproductive systems of both a man and a woman.

"There is a small fee to cover the cost of licensing. This covers the government's time to process the application and the testing and teaching time for the parenting preparation courses. The licensing agreement also contains a provision guaranteeing that each parent would be equally responsible in time for the raising of their child. To make this possible, the government required businesses to accommodate the time pressures on the parents because the growing child is the future of the country and must be cultivated. No weeds can reach the beauty of the tenderly, carefully and intelligently raised rose. We have followed the lead of Norway in this. Norway allows one parent to be released from work for 11 of the first twelve months of life and the other parent can take one month. They are then paid 80 to 100% of their wages by the government. We recommend that the parents alternate months for the first year. The government pays 100% of the wages for this. It is possible for one parent to opt out of this infant raising time. But this has to be done as part of the licensing application.

"If a license is granted, a larger fee of about $5,000 is required. This covers the insurance necessary to care for the child if the parents die, become incapacitated, or are judged to be unfit and the child must be put up for adoption. If one parent is incapacitated or dies and the other parent needs financial aid, it comes from this fund. Since the government is attempting to reduce the country's population, we don't believe that it should be responsible for the day-to-day expenses of child raising. On the other hand, the government pays all expenses of education from pre-school through the doctorate level. Education is our largest national expense. We bring in the best educators we can find and pay exceptionally high salaries. This inspires many foreign educators to come to us. As I mentioned, we allow few outsiders to become citizens, but outstanding educators, along with the outstanding research scientists, are the most likely foreigners to have a chance at citizenship. As our population reduces, if we need more citizens we take them from among those who will help our society the most and will accept our social premises. However if there is any question of equal qualifications of applicants, we always take the applicant from China. After all, China is our mother. We are like the youth who has been allowed to run free, but we always know where we started, where home is.

"As in many other countries, applicants for parent licenses must be checked for a number of communicable and genetic diseases. Positive tests for communicable diseases rules them out until the disease is cured. If they are detected to have genetic diseases it rules out the parent for biological parenthood but not for artificial insemination or adoption. We test for a multitude of genetic problems such as muscular dystrophy, some cancers, and for chromosomal abnormalities as the embryo is developing. We also give a bio-psychological test to ascertain potential brain chemical problems No sense letting the child suffer from something that can be prevented.

"Genes are certainly important. As the late anthropologist Margaret Mead reminded men, 'If you want your children to be bright, you had better marry a bright woman. But, this is an idea that has not occurred to many men.' It seems that intellectual and aesthetic abilities, as well as a number of propensities for psychological traits, are strongly influenced or even controlled by our genes."

"With these tests a married couple might qualify intellectually and psychologically but not physically. They could then get a license to raise a baby, to be an adoptive parent--a psychological parent, but not to have their own biological child. Or, if one of the parents was biologically sound that parent might be able to contribute his or her heredity to the child while using another person as the donor of the other parts of its heredity.

"Another part of the licensing program is to test the potential parents for intelligence. Intelligence tests of various types are also given. Some are paper-pencil tests, other tests measure the speed of electrical currents in the brain to various verbal and electrical stimuli. We also give aptitude and attitude evaluations. We would hope that the potentials and the interests of the parents will expose the children to many life expanding interests.

"Perhaps the most important evaluation is a test for one's ability to love a child unselfishly. We are still developing this evaluative tool. We check the individual's past performance in school and at the job as well as in voluntary work. Since we define parental love as the ability to help the child develop his or her own potentials to the fullest, we want to know whether the parents have been unselfish in the past. Do they have trusted friends. Have they, in the past, shown uncontrollable tempers. In their recreation time has their pleasure come only from their own interests or have they spent some time helping others, such as in youth groups and elder care centers. Have they shown interest in their family members, particularly the younger ones. This unselfish attitude, combined with a knowledge of how a child grows and develops, and an understanding of how to assist a child in becoming the most complete person possible—is our overriding concern.

"The state is very much concerned with helping the parents to expose the child to a myriad of worthwhile experiences, hoping that this exposure will allow the child to develop along the lines that will make his or her life the most enjoyable and productive. It may result in a lifelong occupation or recreational pursuit. We believe that a loving parent should satisfy the child's curiosity, rather than suppressing it."

-- "In my country parents read lots of books on child psychology. They wonder if they did anything right. What else do you do for the growing child?"

--"Smoking is not allowed by either parent during pregnancy and for six months before a conception is planned, by the mother during lactation and neither parent is allowed to smoke in the home. The negative effects of second hand smoke have been documented for years. It is a shame that too many of our citizens still smoke after all the warnings. It seems to be a holdover from the horrible habit we brought with us from China. Babies breathe the cigarette smoke in the air of the home, even if it was their loving mother or father who exhaled that smoke.

"Drinking alcohol is not allowed by either parent for at least one month before the expected conception. Mothers must continue this proscription until they have weaned the child. By requiring this we hope to eliminate alcohol as a damage to sperm and ova before conception and to prevent the fetal alcohol syndrome in the infant. Other psychoactive drugs have not been the problem here that they have been in the West, still we test every parent for drug usage and check for criminal use in the past. Our doctors have found links between some drugs and autism. Other drugs we find to permanently alter the ova. And of course recent use of marijuana can damage the sperm.

"Multiple children are allowed to highly desirable parents who have demonstrated their parental fitness. The honor is also sometimes afforded to world class intellectuals, artists and athletes. But more often to people who have shown exceptional parenting abilities.

"Once the parents have been licensed, the state helps them in every way possible to raise the child. We merely offer aid but do not tell them how to parent. We believe that we have provided them with basic knowledge in the required parenting classes. On getting their license we give them this plaque. I'm sure you've seen it in some form. I just wish I knew who wrote it first. I'd like to give them credit.

--HOW YOUR CHILD LEARNS

If a child lives with criticism, he learns to condemn.
If a child lives with hostility, he learns to fight.
If a child lives with ridicule, he learns to be shy.
If a child lives with shame, he l earns to feel guilty .
If a child lives with tolerance, he learns to be patient.
If a child lives with encouragement, he learns confidence.
If a child lives with praise, he learns to appreciate.
If a child lives with fairness, he learns justice.

If a child lives with security, he learns to have faith.

If a child lives with approval, he learns to like himself.

If a child lives with acceptance and friendship, he learns to find love in the world.

"But our aid doesn't stop there. We inform them weekly of the best information available from the sciences relating to child psychology, nutrition, physiology, diseases and symptoms, how to prevent drug abuse, and so forth. This is done by e-mail and in our newspapers. We also keep them informed of museum exhibits, theater performances, athletic events, youth athletic leagues, special interest groups for children and youth, such as free classes in dance, sports, music appreciation, playing musical instruments and so forth.

"We also have free afternoon and weekend youth centers. These we patterned after the Young Pioneer Palaces of the Soviet Union. This was the best thing that the Russian Communists did. Their huge buildings housed innumerable activities that the child could pursue: ballet, sports, astronomy, physics or chemistry, music composition and performance, tailoring and fashion design, and a number of other activities. To these we have added computer skills, programming, electronic engineering, and other such scientific amusements. We also have special history study, which often includes free trips to the areas studied. Last year the groups that studied ancient Greece as an extracurricular interest were given a trip to Athens, Delphi, Mycenae, Olympia and Troy—which is now in Turkey. We don't have our children wasting their time on playing video games that someone else invented. We believe that developing scientific knowledge, historical or philosophical insights, mastering and instrument or one's voice, or playing sports is a far more enjoyable activity than shooting a monster who is eating Tokyo on your computer screen.

"We strongly encourage breast feeding, but we don't require it as does Singaling. We also emphasize that growing up should be enjoyable. We don't want the parents to push their own agenda on their children. If a father or mother did not reach the highest levels of soccer play, piccolo playing or physics, we don't want them pushing the child to succeed in the void left by the parent."

I told Madam Ching that before I was a space explorer I had been a teacher in Los Angeles. Shortly before I was selected for my solo voyage I had been the football coach at Hollywood High School. Strangely, the most difficult thing to leave in my country was my team. There is something about American football that few people outside of the game understand. My experience in Los Angeles in both junior and senior high schools was that I had not seen one of my pregnant students, whether 13 or 16, who was prepared for parenthood. I would estimate that about 1 in 30 sixteen year olds were pregnant while in my senior high school classes. I concluded that perhaps the licensing requirements of Kino were of a higher order in determining readiness for parenthood than fifteen minutes of condom-free passion in the back seat of a Chevy.

--"Madam President, have you had opposition to your program because it might be genocidal? In my country that would be one of the first objections."

--"No we haven't. We are all Asians here. I can see where you could have that problem in your country, or even if it were proposed for some African countries by Anglos. But here it is Asians reducing the population of Asians. We must look at population control and parent licensing as a human problem, not a racial one. I have no doubt that in the distant future, if the human race survives that long, we will be all one race."

ENFORCEMENT

—"But how could the government of Kino prevent the inevitable products of passion from entering the Kinoese society."

--"Simple, we have developed nearly microscopic plugs that are inserted into the fallopian tubes of infant females and we have small on-off valves that are inserted into the vas deferens of infant males. These devices are not removed until a license for parenthood is obtained. They are reinserted immediately after the birth. Because of these devices we don't have those little 'products of passion' that have graced, or more likely cursed, nearly every society."

-- "And what would happen if a person had these removed and had an unlicensed child?"

--"Simple, the parents would be jailed for fifteen years and would be sterilized while in prison. I have never heard of a couple having a child without a license. Guaranteeing that children have the best parents possible is our highest social aim—and our people understand that.

If people are not licensed here they can go to another country, like the United Colonies, where there is no licensing.

"Another thing we do is that shortly after birth, at the time of the insertion of the birth preventatives, several microscopic chips are shot into the skull of each child. Their whereabouts can always be traced—for their entire lives there is a record. If one were to be a suicide bomber we could tell every place that person had ever gone. We can trace where explosives might have been bought, who they met with, etc. While we rely on ethical values to keep people honest, there are always a few who stray towards criminality. For them the fear of being caught keeps them honest their whole lives. But it is not just the prying Big Brother that those chips aid, but the fraternal Big Brother also. If a person is lost or kidnapped we can find them immediately. If they are unconscious we can get an immediate health report on prior illnesses, drug allergies, and so forth. We can identify our citizens without the aid of passports so illegal immigrants cannot falsify papers.

"We got the idea from your country when you started your Global Positioning System to track sex offenders. You remember that convicted sex offenders had to wear transmitters to satellites that showed exactly where they were 24 hours a day. While your main concern was in preventing future crimes, our intention is two pronged—to prevent problems and to find innocent people who might be victims of accidents, crimes, heart attacks, diabetic comas and so forth.

REWARDS FOR EFFECTIVE PARENTHOOD

"While we make it rather difficult for people to become parents we recognize that their job as parents is often difficult and not always rewarding. But the society recognizes that these people are the builders of our future. They are looked up to because they have passed the difficult licensing and have worked to provide their children, our children, with the opportunity to be loving and successful citizens. To thank them, those who have raised law abiding young adults who have finished their schooling, the society allows them to either take a fully paid vacation of their choice for up to six months or to be given a substantial increase in pay—and often a job promotion.

MEET DR. WANG

"Commander, you wanted to meet Dr. Wang. Here she comes now."

-- "Dr. Wang I'm Commander Gulliver. I have been so excited to meet you. On my odyssey I was able to read much of what you have written. My interest in values parallels yours so

I'd like to talk with you in depth on values. The most important questions we have, the enduring questions of civilization, are questions of values."

--"And basic assumptions, Commander."

--"Of course, basic assumptions. Can we get together tomorrow?"

- "Certainly, Madam Ching has placed me at your disposal during your visit."

--"You look so much like her. You wouldn't be sisters would you?"

--"No, but we are related. Actually we are cousins."

WORLD LEADERSHIP

--"Madam Ching, I can't thank you enough for your company and your filling me in on some of the workings of your country. I can't believe that there is a more forward looking country in the world."

--"Thank you commander for your interest. We may not have all the answers for today's world but we are certainly working on them. It seems that we have that perennial problem of civilizations-- you no sooner solve one problem then three more pop up in your face. But we know this--if you're not riding the wave of change you will be drowned by it. In Kino we have learned to be the surfers of the Bonzai Pipeline of modern living—of technology and social thinking. You must be able to dance a little faster when the orchestra shifts from a waltz to a samba. Our social thinking permeates our society. We have eliminated illegal drugs, largely by executing everyone caught raising, processing, or distributing these drugs. Everyone with an incurable disease, like AIDS, has been sent to a colony where they can live as happily as possible while being separated from the rest of us. We believe that the society that is the most open to new ideas, new technology, and allows for diversity will win the social and economic wars."

—"I had long thought that the high native intelligence and the drive to succeed would someday propel China to leadership in the world. But Kino is definitely leading its mother in this regard. I was just not prepared that it would happen so quickly. One reason was their crashing birthrate which allowed for them to bring in many of the best minds and highest quality business and scientific leaders from other countries."

"Thank you so much for your time. You have enlightened me beyond my expectations. So until we meet again. . . "

NOTES

1. . OECD, Paris. Oct. 23, 2014 https://mail.google.com/mail/u/1/#inbox/1493c4bd01d48650)
2. Sayings of Confucius Ch. 5
3. Mokdad AH et al. "Actual causes of death in the United States, 2000' Journal of American Medical Assn. 291:1238-1245. 2004
4. Sayings of Confucius, Ch 1
5. Sayings of Confucius, Ch 2
6. Aristotle, Politics Bk VI
7. World Bank http://data.worldbank.org/indicator/SP.DYN.TFRT.IN
8. Cauchon, Dennis. "Retiree benefits make 'monster' tax burden: $510,678 per household" USA Today, May 25, 2006
9. Confucius, Sayings, Ch 2